MORE
JOY OF
LEX

GYLES BRANDRETH

MORE JOY OF LEX

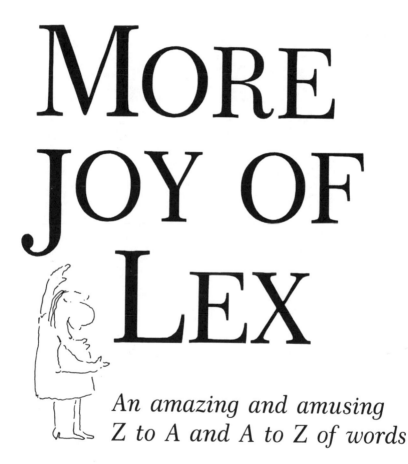

An amazing and amusing
Z to A and A to Z of words

ILLUSTRATED BY GEORGE MORAN

WILLIAM MORROW AND COMPANY, INC.
New York   1982

Library of Congress Cataloging in Publication Data
Brandreth, Gyles Daubeney, 1948-
    More joy of lex.
    1. Word games.   I. Title.
GV1507.W8B684   1982   793.73   82-8127
ISBN 0-688-01338-4   AACR2

Printed in the United States of America
First Edition

1 2 3 4 5 6 7 8 9 10

DESIGN BY BETTY BINNS GRAPHICS

ACKNOWLEDGMENTS

I am greatly indebted to my fellow wordaholics Dave Crossland, Michael Curl, Clive Dickinson, Roger Millington and Peter Newby for their contributions to the book. I would also like to thank Dr. Frederick C. Mish, editorial director of G. and C. Merriam Company, publishers of Merriam-Webster Dictionaries, for his help and for that of his colleagues. Above all I must thank my friend Darryl Francis for his multifarious contributions to the book, several of which were based on articles of his which originally appeared in *Word Ways: The Journal of Recreational Linguistics*, published by Ross Eckler, Morristown, New Jersey.

CONTENTS

MORE JOY OF LEX

INTRODUCTION

No matter how eloquently a dog may bark, he cannot tell you
that his parents were poor but honest.

—BERTRAND RUSSELL

Words and the way we use them are what make us human
animals unique. And words and what we can do with them are
what *More Joy of Lex* is all about. It is a lighthearted celebration of our language—in my view the richest, most diverse,
most exciting and most *entertaining* language in the world.

Even though this book has come about because so many
people seemed to like its predecessor, I still feel a little nervous
about it. Like most authors I'm insecure. I have been ever
since I heard the story of the young writer who wasn't. This

all-too-confident youth plagued a prominent editor with relentless requests to read his latest manuscript. Eventually, and reluctantly, the publisher agreed. Two days later he received a cable from the impatient young writer:

MUST HAVE IMMEDIATE DECISION AS OTHER IRONS IN FIRE.

The publisher wired back:

SUGGEST YOU EXTRACT IRONS AND INSERT MANUSCRIPT.

Whatever I feel about the book as a whole, this one page I'm not worried about because when I was researching *The Joy of Lex* I discovered that 87 percent of readers never look at introductions. Naturally I respect minority groups, which is why I'm gratified you're one of the 13 percent reading this now, but the journey through the amazing and amusing highways and byways of our language really starts across the page.

All the other wordaholics and verbivores are there already. Why don't we join them?

Z TO A AND BACK AGAIN

FROM Z TO A

Welcome to the weird and wonderful world of words, a world that depends for its existence entirely on the letters of the alphabet, each one of which happens to be a word in its own right.

Some letters even have several meanings. Here are just twenty-six of them:

Z   A buzzing sound.

Y   A principal railroad track and two diverging branches arranged like the letter Y.

X   A mistake or error.

W   A printer's type for reproducing the letter W.

V   A V-shaped neck of a dress, sweater or blouse.

U   Characteristic of the upper classes.

T	An offensive soccer formation.
S	A grade assigned by a teacher rating a student's work as satisfactory.
R	One of the three Rs (writing, reading and arithmetic).
Q	The ratio of the reactance to the resistance of an oscillatory circuit.
P	The chemical symbol for phosphorus.
O	Zero.
N	An indefinite number.
M	An antigen of human blood that shares a common genetic locus with the N antigen.
L	An elevated railroad.
K	In mathematics, a unit vector parallel to the z-axis.
J	In mathematics, a unit vector parallel to the y-axis.
I	An excessively egotistic person.
H	Something having the shape of the letter H.
G	A sum of 1000 dollars.
F	A grade assigned by a teacher rating a student's work as so inferior as to be failing.
E	The second class Lloyd's rating for the quality of a merchant ship.
D	A semicircle on a pool table that is about twenty-two inches in diameter and is used especially in snooker games.
C	A sum of 100 dollars.
B	A motion picture produced on a small budget and usually shown as a supplement to the main feature.
A	A chiefly Scots form of *all*.

FROM A TO Z

If you didn't care for those words, try these:

A	A major blood group.
B	In men's pajama sizes, medium.

C	The cardinal number of the set of all real numbers.
D	A proportional brassiere cup size, smaller than DD and larger than C.
E	A flag bearing the letter E, for "efficiency," presented during World War II as an award by the army or navy to factories meeting or passing their production schedules of war materials.
F	The medieval Roman numeral for 40.
G	The fifth tone in the scale of C major, or the seventh tone in the relative minor scale, A minor.
H	The horizontal component of the Earth's magnetic field.
I	The imaginary number that is the square root of minus 1.
J	The medieval Roman numeral for 1.
K	In computer technology, the number 1000 or 1024.
L	An extension at right angles to one end of a building.
M	A printing unit.
N	In optics, the index of refraction.
O	The exclamation *oh*.
P	In music, softly.
Q	In Biblical criticism, the symbol for material common to the gospels of Matthew and Luke that was not derived from the gospel of Mark.
R	Are (as in "oysters R in season").
S	The energy state of an electron in an atom having an orbital angular momentum of zero.
T	The relation between points and closed sets in topological space.
U	A Burmese title of respect applied to a man.
V	The symbol of allied victory in World War II.
W	The twenty-third in order.
X	A film recommended for adults only.
Y	In mathematics, the y-axis.
Z	The medieval Roman numeral for 2000.

TWO'S COMPANY

And if single-letter words leave you cold, don't worry. Most of the words in the book are a little longer—like these:

aa	A type of volcanic lava.
ag	Relating to agriculture.
ai	A South American sloth.
bu	A Japanese coin.
da	A heavy Burmese knife.
dy	A type of sediment deposited in some lakes.
ea	A stream.
fu	An administrative division of China and Japan.
fy	An interjection.
gi	A costume worn for judo or karate.
gu	A kind of violin used in the Shetland Islands of Scotland.
ie	A mat or basket made from a certain type of fiber.
io	A large hawk from Hawaii.
ix	The axle of a cart or wagon.
jo	A sweetheart.
ka	A personality double.
ki	Any of several Asian and Pacific trees.
li	A Chinese unit of measure.
ob	An objection.
od	A force.
oe	A whirlwind.
om	A mantra.
oo	An extinct Hawaiian bird.
ri	A Japanese unit of measure.
sy	A chiefly dialectal spelling of *scythe*.
ug	A feeling of disgust.
vi	A Polynesian tree.
yi	In Chinese philosophy, the faithful performance of one's specified duties to society.

yu   Jade.

zo   A type of Asian cattle.

FROM ALOHA TO ZIZZ

These twenty-six words are longer still, and what's interesting about them is that each one begins and ends with the same letter.

aloha	*Jernej*	*syllables*
blob	*kick*	*tot*
cynic	*lull*	*unau*
dad	*mum*	*valv*
ewe	*neon*	*wow*
fluff	*octavo*	*Xerox*
grinning	*pop*	*yolky*
health	*Qaraqalpaq*	*zizz*
iambi	*razor*	

Iambi is the plural of *iambus,* part of a line of poetry having two syllables; *Jernej* is a Yugoslavian forename; *Qaraqalpaq* is a Turkic people of Central Asia; *unau* is an animal, a type of sloth; *valv* is a reformed spelling of *valve.*

WORD CHAIN CHALLENGE

Think of a word beginning with A and ending with B. Think of a word beginning with B and ending with C. Think of a word beginning with C and ending with D. And go on right through the alphabet. Any word will do to fill each gap. How far can you get before you run into trouble? As far as I—J in my case. Look:

a—b	*adverb*	c—d	*cold*
b—c	*basic*	d—e	*dove*

e—f	*elf*	p—q	???
f—g	*flag*	q—r	*queer*
g—h	*girth*	r—s	*rats*
h—i	*Hindi*	s—t	*sit*
i—j	???	t—u	*tableau*
j—k	*junk*	u—v	???
k—l	*kill*	v—w	*vow*
l—m	*loom*	w—x	*wax*
m—n	*moon*	x—y	*xerography*
n—o	*nuncio*	y—z	*yez*
o—p	*overlap*	z—a	*zebra*

There are three gaps (i—j, p—q, and u—v). These can all be filled by choosing uncommon proper names. For example, *Igej* is a town in Hungary, and *Inathganj* is a place in Pakistan; *Pontacq* is a wine from the south of France; and *Ulanov* and *Ushpitov* are towns in the USSR. *Yez*, by the way, is an Anglo-Irish pronoun meaning "you" in the plural.

A TO Z IN THE MIDDLE

Here are three lists of words. In each list, the middle letters of the words run from *A* to *Z*. In the case of the seven-letter words, the first three letters and the last three letters also form words; in the case of the nine-letter words, the first four letters and the last four letters also form words; and in the case of the eleven-letter words, the first five letters and the last five letters form words. Unfortunately examples of nine and eleven-letter words with a Q in the middle are missing. Yes, even in *More Joy of Lex* there are going to be occasional disappointments.

7 LETTERS	9 LETTERS	11 LETTERS
carAvan	bungAlows	blockAdings
jawBone	rainBowed	underBought
teaCher	blueCoats	extraCtable
banDits	snowDrift	screwDriver

7 LETTERS	9 LETTERS	11 LETTERS
vetEran	bothEring	adultEratcd
warFare	goldFinch	satinFlower
bagGage	kiloGrams	underGround
witHout	brigHtens	unrigHtable
manIkin	handIwork	deterIorate
conJure	flapJacks	interJangle
weeKend	sparKling	underKeeled
lowLand	paneLwork	oversLoping
barMaid	clayMores	blackMailed
furNace	lameNtory	heaveNwards
bayOnet	bestOwing	trampOlines
ramPart	tramPling	enterPrises
ubiQuit	???	???
curRant	mayoRship	butteRflies
penSion	brimStone	sweepStakes
vanTage	sideTrack	forgeTtable
butUmen	consUlate	prestUdying
canVass	disaVowed	extraVagate
hogWash	bushWomen	lightWeight
manXman	trioXides	overeXpress
copYcat	pansYlike	staphYlions
manZana	waltZlike	hydraZonium

THE A TO Z OF LIFE

And if you still can't remember the letters of the alphabet, here's an ABC to help you.

ABC	Always Be Careful
DEF	Don't Ever Forget
GHI	Go Home Immediately
JKL	Just Keep Looking
MNO	Miss No Opportunities

PQR	Prevent Quarrels at Recess
STU	Stop Talking Unnecessarily
VWX	Verify With X Rays
YZ	You're a Zany!

YOUR VERY GOOD HEALTH

If you need an excuse for a drink, you are going to like this chapter. It's the only one in the book I won't allow you to read until you have a drink in your hand—albeit an innocent glass of orange juice. Not only do I want you to enjoy yourself with some liquid refreshment before reading any further, I also want you to read the chapter standing up. Why? Because, ladies and gentlemen, I am about to propose a toast—or to be more accurate I'm about to propose fifteen—so I hope you've got strong legs and you're feeling thirsty.

Once upon a time, when a toast was proposed it was done with wit and charm and style. That isn't true anymore and it's because I want to revive the best of the good old days that I'd like to introduce you to my all-time favorite toasts. Whatever the occasion—a banquet at the White House, a wedding anniversary, a modest meal with two or three friends—you should be able to find something here to fit the bill. So, without more ado, would you kindly raise your glasses and be upstanding, for the Toasts:

1 To your good health, old friend,
  may you live for a thousand years,
  and I be there to count them.

2 May your joys be as deep as the ocean
  and your sorrows as light as its foam.

3 Drink not to my past, which is
      weak and indefensible,
  Nor to my present, which is not
      above reproach;
  But let us drink to our futures, which,
      thank God, are immaculate.

4 Here's wishing you the kind of troubles
  that will last as long as your New Year's resolutions!

5 Here's to the lasses we've loved, my lad,
  Here's to the lips we've pressed;
  For of kisses and lasses
  Like liquor in glasses,
  The last is always the best.

6 Here's to the bride that is to be,
  Happy and smiling and fair,
  Here's to those who would like to be
  And wondering when and where.

7 May I present you to a person who knows
  all there is to know about banks except breaking
  and entering.

8 Here's champagne to our real friends,
  and real pain to our sham friends.

9 Drink! for you know not whence you come, nor why:
  Drink! for you know not why you go, nor where.

10 Drink to me only with thine eyes,
      And I will pledge with mine;
   Or leave a kiss but in the cup
      And I'll not look for wine.

11 Here's to matrimony, the high sea for which
   no compass has yet been invented.

12 Here's to the red of the holly berry,
   And to its leaf so green;
   And here's to the lips that are just as red,
   And the fellow who's not so green.

13 The Ladies—We admire them for their beauty,
   respect them for their intelligence, adore them
   for their virtue, and love them because we
   can't help it.

14 May friendship, like wine, improve as time
   advances, and may we always have old wine,
   old friends, and young cares.

I've left my favorite toast till last. It was first proposed by Mark Twain.

15 Let us toast the fools; but for them
   the rest of us could not succeed.

X MARKS THE SPOT

THE JOY OF X

I like some letters of the alphabet much more than others. My analyst—if I had one—could probably tell me why, but I can't. All I know is that I don't care much for J and R, but X I just adore!

Xan is my son's second name and X is the first letter I turn to when I open a new dictionary. Everyone is familiar with xylophone and X ray and xenophobia, but there are many more intriguing words that begin with X. Here are thirty of my favorites:

xanorphica	A stringed musical instrument.
Xanthippe	An ill-tempered woman.
xanthocyanopsy	Color blindness in which the ability to distinguish only yellow and blue is present, vision for red being wanting.

xanthoderm	A person with yellow skin.
xarque	Jerked meat.
xat	A carved pole erected as a memorial to the dead by some Indians of western North America.
xebec	A Mediterranean sailing ship.
xenagogue	A guide.
xenalasy	The banishment of aliens from ancient Sparta by official action.
xenia	Gifts sometimes given compulsorily to medieval rulers and churches.
xenodogheionology	The lore of hotels and inns.
xeriff	A gold coin, at one time current in Turkey and Egypt.
xerophagy	The eating of dry food.
xerosis	Abnormal dryness of a body.
xibalba	In Maya religion, the abode of the dead.
xicaque	An Indian people of northern Honduras.
xilinous	Of cotton.
xiphoid	Sword-shaped.
xoanon	A primitive image carved in wood.
xu	A monetary unit of North Vietnam.
xurel	A fish.
xya	A genus of mole-crickets, mainly tropical.
xylanthrax	Charcoal.
xyloglyphy	Artistic wood carving.
xylomancy	Divination by means of pieces of wood.
xylopolist	A timber merchant.
xylosistron	A musical instrument.
xysma	Membranous shreds in the stools of patients with diarrhea or dysentery.
xyster	An instrument for scraping bones.
xystus	A walk lined with trees.

THE CRUX OF THE MATTER

There are many more words that end with X than start with it. I have scoured the dictionaries to come up with twenty-six of the longest, each beginning with a different letter of the alphabet. Some of the definitions are obvious, but several are quite as obscure as the words themselves. So if you want them I'll leave you to leaf through the pages of the 1934 and 1961 editions of *Webster's* unabridged.

archcystosyrinx
blennothorax
coadministratrix
dispensatrix
erysipalothrix
fornicatrix
glossenthrax
hydropneumothorax
impersonatrix
janitrix
knisteneaux
lithanthrax
metrosalpinx
negotiatrix
odontopteryx
pneumohydrothorax
quadruplex
rickettsialpox
seropneumothorax
trophothylax
ultraorthodox
versificatrix
wheelbox
xylanthrex
yunx
zelatrix

THE JOY OF LEX

If X is my favorite letter, *lex* is almost my favorite three-letter word. I reckon there are about fifty words in the English language that begin with the letters *L, E, X*. Here are thirty of them:

Lexa	A town in Arkansas.
Lexden	A town in Essex, England.
lexeme	A meaningful speech form that is an item of the vocabulary of a language.
lexemic	Relating to a lexeme.
lexer	A student of law.
lexia	A soft raisin produced chiefly in Spain and Australia.
lexica	A plural of *lexicon*.
lexical	Relating to words or the vocabulary of a language.
lexicalize	To accept into the vocabulary of a language.
lexicographer	A dictionary compiler.
lexicographian	Relating to lexicography.
lexicographical	Relating to lexicography.
lexicography	The principles and practices of dictionary making.
lexicological	Relating to lexicology.
lexicologist	One versed in lexicology.
lexicology	The science of the derivation and significance of words.
lexicon	A dictionary or word-stock.
lexiconist	A compiler of a lexicon.
lexiconize	To make a lexicon.
lexicostatistic	Pertaining to the statistics of vocabulary.
lexigram	Any figure or symbol used to represent a word.
lexigraphic	Pertaining to lexigraphy.
lexigraphy	The art or practice of defining words.

Lexington	A town in Massachusetts, the site of the first engagement of the American Revolution.
lexiphanes	A phrase monger.
lexiphanic	Pretentious.
lexiphanicism	Pretentious phraseology.
lexipharmic	An antidote.
lexis	The wording of a piece of writing.

And here are the last three letters of thirty words that end with L, E, X. Can you work out how the words should begin? (See Answers.)

_ _ _ _ _ lex	To strike with a sudden loss of consciousness.
_ _ _ _ _ _ _ lex	An accent mark.
_ _ _ _ lex	Complicated.
_ _ lex	A genus of mosquitoes.
_ _ _ _ _ _ lex	Having ten parts.
_ _ _ lex	Twofold.
_ _ lex	Without legal authority.
_ lex	To bend.
_ _ _ _ _ _ _ lex	10 raised to the power of a googol.
_ _ _ lex	Man's great toe.
_ lex	An evergreen oak of southern Europe.
· _ _ _ lex	Intricate.
_ _ _ _ _ _ lex	Having numerous parts.
_ _ _ _ _ lex	Relating to a system of telegraphy in which eight messages can be sent simultaneously.
_ _ _ _ lex	To bewilder.
_ lex	To make like a network.
_ _ _ lex	Thumb.
_ _ _ _ lex	A complicated network of nerves.

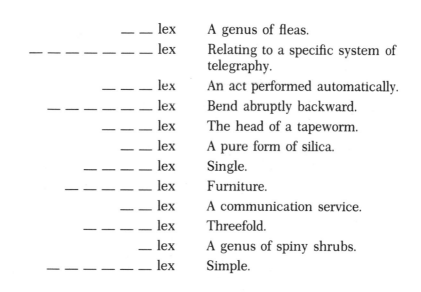

_ _ lex	A genus of fleas.
_ _ _ _ _ _ _ lex	Relating to a specific system of telegraphy.
_ _ _ lex	An act performed automatically.
_ _ _ _ _ _ lex	Bend abruptly backward.
_ _ _ lex	The head of a tapeworm.
_ _ lex	A pure form of silica.
_ _ _ _ lex	Single.
_ _ _ _ _ lex	Furniture.
_ _ lex	A communication service.
_ _ _ _ lex	Threefold.
_ lex	A genus of spiny shrubs.
_ _ _ _ _ _ lex	Simple.

COMPLEX ARRANGEMENTS

Here are thirty more words that don't seem to have anything to do with Lex—yet. This is where you come in. Take each word in turn, add the letters *L*, *E* and *X*, and rearrange all the letters to make a new word. For example, if *TO* was in the list, add the letters *LEX*, rearrange all five, and make the new word EX-TOL. Simple, isn't it?

at	flyer	ropiest
coin	goosy	seat
cosier	hi	shop
cued	hoof	sienna
dart	linky	snary
date	lot	sup
dope	mawl	taut
due	pain	ties
eater	pore	upset
fan	read	us

(See Answers.)

TWO OUT OF THREE

You can change the vowel in the middle of *lex* and come up with four other useful words:

lax   Not strict.

lix   A Roman camp follower.

lox   Liquid oxygen.

lux   In physics, a unit of illumination.

(Not to mention *lyx,* which is a combining form, related to the chemical lyxosa.)

If you want to change the last letter of lex and come up with a series of alternative three-letter words, each beginning with a different letter of the alphabet, you can—if you don't mind ignoring Q and including slang, abbreviations, dialect, proper names and obsolete words galore.

lea	Pasture.
lab	As much liquid or food as can be taken into the mouth or thrown by the hand at one time.
lec	An obsolete spelling of *leek.*
led	The past tense of *lead.*
lee	The side sheltered from the wind.
lef	An obsolete spelling of *leaf, leave, lief,* and *live.*
leg	A limb.
Leh	A commercial town in Ladakh province, Kashmir.
lei	A Polynesian garland of flowers.
lej	An abbreviation for *longitudinal expansion joint.*
lek	A site to which birds regularly resort for the purposes of sexual display and courtship.
lel	An obsolete spelling of *leal,* "loyal."
LEM	Lunar excursion module.
Len	Short for *Leonard.*
Leo	The fifth sign of the zodiac.
lep	A dialectal spelling of *lap* and *leap.*
leq	???

Ler The Irish god of the sea, the original of King Lear.

les An obsolete spelling of *lace, lease, leash,* and *less.*

let Allow.

leu The basic monetary unit of Romania.

lev The basic monetary unit of Bulgaria.

lew A place of shelter.

lex Law.

ley Pasture.

lez Lesbian.

Running through the alphabet looking for three-letter words ending in *ex* isn't so easy.

Aex A genus of short-legged perching duck.

bex An obsolete plural of *beak.*

cex An obsolete spelling of *six.*

Dex A diminutive form of the masculine forename Dexter.

eex ???

fex A variant spelling of *fax,* the hair on the head.

gex An English dialect word meaning "to guess."

hex A spell or jinx.

iex ???

Jex A surname, related to Geake and Jacks.

kex The dry stalk of various plants.

lex Law.

Mex A Mexican.

nex An obsolete spelling of *next.*

OEX An abbreviation for the Office of Educational Exchange.

pex An obsolete spelling of *pax,* peace.

qex ???

rex King.

sex Gender.

Tex A nickname for Texas or someone from Texas.

uex An obsolete spelling of *vex.*

vex To worry.

wex   A dialectal spelling of *wax.*

xex   ???

yex   To hiccup.

zex   A variant spelling of *sax,* a chopping tool for trimming slates.

It seems we don't yet have meanings for *eex, iex, qex* and *xex.* I believe we ought to have. Perhaps *eex* should be the first spouse of a twice-divorced person, *iex* an English form of "Eureka!," *qex* someone who gets kicks out of spelling badly and *xex* be a point on the map . . . as in "xex marks the spot." If you have any deft definitions of your own, tell your friends. I think we should all do what we can here to spread the words.

WHAT'S IN A NAME?

WHAT AM I?

If you don't know who you are, I can't help you. But if you don't know *what* you are, perhaps I can. I know what I am.

Gyles is quite simply the plural form of gyle, and depending on the dictionary you care to consult, gyle is defined as:

—wort in the process of fermentation added to a stout or ale.
—the beer produced at one brewing.
—a quantity of beer brewed at one time.
—a brewing.
—the vat in which the wort is left to ferment.
—an obsolete spelling of *guile*.

—a channel on a beach that the high tide fills, leaving a small island within.

—an island of sand.

—quicksand.

—a ravine, a narrow valley or glen, with precipitous or rocky banks, generally wooded and with a stream running at the bottom.

—a dingle.

—a rivulet or mountain stream.

—the bed of a stream.

—a waterfall.

—a ditch.

And brandreth is variously defined as:

—a gridiron.

—a tripod or trivet of iron.

—a wooden framework for support, as a stand for a small haystack.

—a framework of wood for various purposes, as a stand for a cask.

—a substructure of piles to support a house.

—a fence or rail around the opening of a well.

—an iron framework placed over or before a fire, on which to rest utensils in cooking.

—an iron grating or brazier in which fire is kindled in the open air.

—a wooden or iron arm fixed into the throat of a spindle in a flour mill.

—one of the cross-timbers in a pit, to which slides are bolted.

—a grating placed over the entrance of a drain or sewer.

—the name of a mountain in Cumberland, England, which is 2,344 feet high.

—the name of a community in Herkimer County, New York, named, I believe, after my great-great-grandfather, who marketed Brandreth's Pills, a medicine that could cure almost anything—from headache to heart disease—and made him a fortune. (All since gone, I'm sorry to say.)

Of course, I'm not alone. Numerous surnames have meanings as ordinary words—I know a Butcher and a Baker and I believe there's a man in Florida called Hans Candlestickmaker—and there are plenty of forenames that are also words in their own right. For example, Jenny is a female bird or animal, especially a female donkey; Jemima is an elastic-sided boot; Mike is short for *microphone;* and Will is a document bequeathing one's possessions at death.

Here, with definitions, are more than a hundred of them. I hope you find your name in the list.

Abigail	A lady's maid.
Albert	A short kind of watch chain.
Alma	An Egyptian dancing girl.
Ann	From 1672 to 1925, a half-year's stipend payable to the wife of a parish minister after his death.
Anna	An obsolescent coin of India and Pakistan.
Basil	An aromatic plant.
Ben	A mountain peak.
Beryl	A precious stone.
Bertha	A woman's falling collar.
Beth	The second letter of the Hebrew alphabet.
Betty	A burglar's jimmy.
Bill	A bird's beak.
Billy	An Australian teapot.
Bob	To move up and down.
Bobby	A policeman.
Carol	A Christmas song.
Cicely	The name of several plants.
Clement	Mild.
Clementine	A type of orange.
Colin	The Virginian quail.
Craig	A crag, a rough steep rock or point.
Dan	A box for carrying coal.
Dick	A detective.
Dickens	The devil.
Dicky	A false shirtfront.
Dolly	A trolley.

Don	To put on.
Emma	A signaler's name for the letter *M*.
Eric	A murderer's fine in old Irish law.
Faith	Confidence.
Fay	A fairy.
Flora	The vegetation of a region.
Frank	Open.
Grace	Favor.
Guy	An odd figure or fellow.
Hank	A loop.
Harry	To harass.
Hazel	Light brown.
Heather	A common shrub.
Henry	In physics, the unit of inductance.
Iris	Part of the eye.
Ivy	An evergreen climbing plant.
Jack	A device for raising heavy weights.
Jake	A country lout.
James	A burglar's jimmy.
Jane	A woman.
Jean	A twilled cotton cloth.
Jeff	In circus slang, a rope.
Jerry	A chamber pot.
Jess	A short strap around the legs of a hawk.
Jill	A female ferret.
Jo	A beloved one.
Josy	A young kangaroo.
Josh	To ridicule.
Ken	To know.
Kirk	A church.
Laura	A group of recluses' cells.
Louis	An old French gold coin.
Luke	Tepid.
Madge	A magpie.

Maria	Dark areas on the moon and Mars.
Martin	A bird.
Matt	Dull.
Molly	A milksop.
Mona	A West African monkey.
Mungo	Waste cloth.
Nelly	A large petrel, a type of bird.
Nelson	A wrestling hold.
Nick	To steal.
Norma	A rule or standard.
Norman	A bar inserted in a windlass
Olive	A tree with oily fruit.
Oliver	A forge hammer worked by hand.
Otto	A fragrant oil.
Pansy	The name of various plants.
Patrick	A seventeenth-century Irish halfpenny.
Patty	A little pie.
Paul	An obsolete papal silver coin.
Peggy	A small warbler, a type of bird.
Peter	To dwindle away.
Polly	A tube of mineral water.
Rex	Pranks.
Rob	To plunder.
Robin	A bird with a red-orange breast.
Rose	Got up.
Rosemary	A small fragrant shrub.
Ruby	A highly prized stone.
Ruth	Pity.
Sally	To rush out suddenly.
Sam	Together.
Saul	A Scots form of *soul*.
Sophia	Divine wisdom.
Taffy	Flattery.
Ted	To spread new-mown grass for drying.

Terry	A pile fabric.
Timothy	A grass for feeding cattle.
Toby	Robbery on the road.
Tommy	A private in the British army.
Tony	Fashionable.
Victor	A winner.
Wally	Excellent.
Watt	In physics, a unit of power.

AN ORAL DANGER

"An oral danger" is, of course, an anagram of *Ronald Reagan*. Less controversial—and less telling—are these anagrams of my name:

Bet her dry slang

Beth's grand lyre

Blyth's gardener

Brash, dry, gentle

Brethren lag Syd

Dr. Glen's breathy

Dry angel berths

Gentry held bars

Gentry's halberd

Grab thy lenders

Hags blend Terry

Harry gets blend

Lady G's brethren

Lend gray berths

Lengthy red bars

Set herb grandly

Sh! Tangled berry

St. Henry garbled

Tangle dry herbs

The berry glands

The dry barn legs

The Gerry's bland

The grand beryls

Try garbled hens

Curiously a great number of forenames are anagrams of other forenames. Look at these:

Christiaan, Christiana

Carla, Clara

Adina, Aidan, Nadia, Naida

Adna, Anda, Dana, Nada

Alvina, Lavina

Armina, Marian, Marina

Anita, Tania

Ramona, Romana

Abbe, Babe, Ebba

Barend, Braden, Brande, Brenda

Bernard, Brander

Brady, Darby

Embla, Mabel, Mable, Melba

Albert, Bartel, Bartle

Bat, Tab

Meriadoc, Mordecai

Alice, Celal, Celia

Caroline, Cornelia

Christian, Christina

Carlo, Carol, Coral

Claus, Lucas

Darel-Gene, Geraldene

Darleen, Darlene, Leander, Leandre, Learned

Dorothea, Theodora

Leandro, Leonard

Dean, Dena, Edan, Edna

Waldorf, Walford

Lorinda, Rinaldo, Rolinda

Arnoldo, Orlando

Arnold, Landor, Nordal, Roland, Roldan, Ronald

Rosamond, Rosmonda

Andy, Dyna

Stanhope, Stephano

Antoine, Antonie

Jane, Jean

Paulet, Petula

Earl, Lear

Amery, Marye

Warner, Warren

Zane, Zena

Etta, Tate

Gary, Gray

Hatty, Hyatt

Oliva, Viola

Marion, Morina

Mario, Moira

Ian, Ina

Nita, Tina

Lawton, Walton

Norma, Ramon, Roman

Amor, Mora, Omar, Roma

Mary, Myra

Mat, Tam

Amy, May

Ann, Nan

Bert, Bret

Cheri, Erich

Colin, Nicol

Dorothee, Theodore

Delores, Delrose

Edsel, Leeds

Fidel, Field

Dolly, Lloyd

Dot, Tod

Esther, Hester

Ernie, Irene, Renie

Elmer, Merle

Simeon, Simone

Len, Nel

Elon, Leon, Noel, Olen

Believe it or not, the list as given here is arranged in a very specific order. It is *not* a random ordering. It is obviously not alphabetically ordered, nor ordered by length. Can you determine the way in which the list of names has been ordered? (See Answers.)

V
ERBIGERATION

Verbigeration is something I hope I'm not guilty of as a paid-up member of Wordaholics Anonymous. Do you know what it means? I do, but only because I looked it up in *Webster's Third New International Dictionary*, where I found fifty different words connected in some way with the study of words and language, writing, and speech.

Here are the fifty words:

1 agnomen	7 caconym
2 anaphora	8 caesura
3 antiphrasis	9 calque
4 asyndeton	10 carriwitchet
5 billingsgate	11 cheville
6 boustrophedon	12 chrestomathy

13 coprolalia	32 neolalia
14 ambolalia	33 neoterism
15 enclitic	34 onomasiology
16 epexegesis	35 onomasticon
17 epistrophe	36 onomatomania
18 equivoke	37 orismology
19 etymon	38 palilalia
20 euonym	39 paralalia
21 euphuism	40 paraphrasia
22 gradus	41 parasynthesis
23 hapax	42 paroemiology
24 heteroclitic	43 paronym
25 idioglossia	44 paronomasia
26 incipit	45 periphrasis
27 isogloss	46 pleonasm
28 jussive	47 schizophasia
29 koine	48 semanteme
30 macaronic	49 tmesis
31 metonymy	50 verbigeration

And here are fifty definitions, but the definitions aren't given in the same order as the words. What you've got to do is match the words to the definitions. If you get as many as thirty correctly matched, you're obviously a dedicated verbivore. If you manage forty, you're probably a lexicographer by profession. And if you get all fifty right, you should be writing the book, not me.

A   A collection or listing of proper names of persons or places.

B   A play upon words in which the same word is used in different senses, or words similar in sound are set in opposition so as to give antithetical force.

C   Speech especially of a psychotic that includes words that are new and meaningless to the hearer.

D   The study of words and expressions having similar or associated concepts for being grouped.

E   The subject of proverbs.

F   A word formed from a word in another language.

G   Uncontrollable obsession with words or names or their meanings or their sounds.

H   A newly invented word or phrase.

I   A word or a base that expresses a definite image or idea.

J   A speech disorder marked by distortions of sounds or substitutions of letters.

K   A composition characterized by a mixture of vernacular words with Latin words or with non-Latin words having Latin endings.

L   Continual repetition of stereotyped phrases, as in schizophrenia.

M   A speech defect marked by abnormal repetition of syllables, words, or phrases.

N   The disorganized speech characteristic of schizophrenia.

O   The science of defining technical terms.

P   Speech defect characterized by incoherence in arrangement of words.

Q   The use of a longer phrasing in place of a possible shorter and plainer form of expression.

R   Separation of parts of a compound word by the intervention of one or more words.

S   A break in the flow of sound in a line of verse, occasioned usually by a rhetorical pause and occurring usually at about the middle of the verse.

T   A noun irregular in declension.

U   The use of more words than those necessary to denote mere sense.

V   A figure of speech that consists of using the name of one thing for that of something else with which it is associated.

W   The process of word formation by adding a derivative ending and prefixing a particle (as in *denationalize*).

X   A word or form evidenced by a single citation.

Y   The writing of alternate lines in opposite directions, one line from left to right and the next from right to left.

Z   The interpolation of meaningless sounds or words into speech.

AA Obsessive or uncontrollable use of obscene language.

BB Repetition of the same word or expression at the end of successive phrases, clauses, or sentences for rhetorical effect.

CC Repetition of a word or words at the beginning of two or more successive clauses or verses for rhetorical or poetic effect.

DD An explanation following a word or larger part of a text that limits its application or clarifies its meaning.

EE A word or particle treated in pronunciation as forming part of the preceding word (as English *thee* in *prithee* and *not* in *cannot*).

FF A linguistic feature shared by some but not all speakers of a dialect, a language, or a group of related languages.

GG A linguistic borrowing that consists of the imitation in one language in some part of the peculiar range of meaning of a particular word in another language.

HH The use of words in senses opposite to the generally accepted meanings or the use of a word in this way usually for humorous or ironical purposes.

II A condition in which the affected person pronounces his words so badly as to speak a language of his own.

JJ A taxonymic name that is objectionable for linguistic reasons.

KK A hoaxing or riddling question.

LL A selection of passages from various authors compiled as an aid to learning a language.

MM A redundant word or phrase used to fill out a sentence or verse.

NN A word, form, case, or mood expression command.

OO Wordplay.

PP The introductory words or part of a medieval manuscript or early printed book.

QQ An affected style of conversation and writing fashionable in the time of Queen Elizabeth I of England and characterized by antithesis alliteration, similes, and a pervading striving for elegance.

RR A dictionary of Greek or Latin prosody and poetical phrases formerly used as an aid in the writing of poetry in Greek or Latin.

SS A name well suited to the person, place, or thing named.

TT A dialect or language of a region, country, or people that has become the common or standard language of a larger area and of other peoples.

UU The original form of a word either in the same language or in an ancestral language.

VV An additional name or epithet.

WW Condemnatory language marked by the coarse or offensive and scornfully abusive or contentious.

XX Omission of the conjunctions that ordinarily join coordinate words or clauses.

(See Answers.)

U NCLES AND AUNTS

It is a mistake to try to put on your uncles and aunts when you are already wearing your Oscar Hocks and your bottles of booze. Your storm and strife will think you're elephant trunk again!

And if that didn't make much sense to you, don't worry. It's in Rhyming Slang, a jargon with an exhilarating, if limited, vocabulary that has been used in America, Australia, and Britain for over a hundred years. If you feel like adding a little color to your everyday language, you could try adopting a few of these unusual but useful words and phrases. All are in current use.

apple and banana	piano
applepies	eyes
bacon and eggs	legs
bar of soap	dope

ben flake	steak
big bloke	coke (short for *cocaine*)
bonny fair	hair
bottles of booze	shoes
bowl of chalk	talk
brothers and sisters	whiskers
bull's aunts	pants
by the peck	neck
Catherine Hayes	long days
chair and cross	horse
Charlie Beck	check
Charlie Chalk	talk
Charlie Horner	corner
Charlie Rocks	socks
cocked hat	rat (an informer)
cracks-a-cry	die
daisy roots	boots
Danny Rucker	butter
Dan O'Leary	weary
dig and dirt	shirt
dime a pop	cop
east-and-west	vest
elephant trunk	drunk
fiddle and flute	suit
fifteen and seven	heaven (enjoyable)
fine and dandy	brandy
fleas and ants	pants
frog a log	dog
garlic and glue	stew
ginger ale	jail
grocery store	door
hair and brain	chain
hairy float	coat
hammer and tack	back (of the body)

hard and flat	hat
heart and lung	tongue
heavenly bliss	kiss
here and there	chair
hook of mutton	button
I declare	chair
in the sleet	in the street
ivory float	coat
Jack O'Brien	train
Jack Scratch	match
Jerry McGinn	chin
Jimmy Hope	soap
Johnnie Rump	pump
Johnnie O'Brien	iron
Johnnie Russell	hustle
Jollopp	stop
Kelly Ned	head
Kennedy Rot	sot
Kentucky horn	corn
kiss the cross	the boss
lard and pail	jail
leg-rope	hope
made mile	smile
moan and wail	jail
mother and daughter	water
mumbley pegs	legs
Nancy prance	dance
new south	mouth
Oh heck	neck
ones and twos	shoes
Oscar Hocks	socks
Oscar Joes	toes
pair of braces	races

peaches and pears	stairs
pint pot	sot
pot of jelly	belly
quarter pot	sot
rattle and jar	car
raw and ripe	pipe
red steer	beer
ride plush	to hush
rise and shine	wine
roasty roast	post (winning)
rocks and boulders	shoulders
rolley roar	floor
roots	boots
roses red	bed
ruby rose	nose
rumble and shock	knock (on the door)
satin and silk	milk
scarlet pips	lips
scream and holler	dollar
see the shine	give a dime
sheery flips	lips
sighs and tears	ears
silk and top	cop
silk and twine	wine
slick and sleeth	teeth
smack in the eye	pie
smear and smudge	judge
south of the equator	elevator
spinning top	cop
stand an ale	go bail (for)
storm and strife	wife
strong and thin	gin
stump the chalk	walk

sweet Margaret	cigarette
switch and bone	telephone
tar and feather	weather
tarry rope	dope
tea and tattle	battle
tears and cheers	ears
thick and dense	expense
three or four	door
tick tack	track
ting-a-ling	ring
tip and tap	cap
toad in the hole	roll of currency notes
Tommy Rocks	socks
Tommy Toy	boy
Tom Noddy	body
train wreck	neck
uncles and aunts	pants
unders and beneaths	teeth
very best	chest
whale and gale	jail
wish me luck	duck (dodge or escape)
you know	snow (cocaine)

T
ERSE VERSE

Poetic License

If you write a long sentence with few capitals and little punctuation,

> then write down
> short phrases
> like lists,
> is it poetry?

No, never, you answer firmly. And I used to agree with you until I came across the vital verses of Alan F. G. Lewis, the world's greatest punster. If this isn't poetry, what is?

Valentine Rhyme

My heart and I
Call to you
But you're too deaf
to Eros.

Please Be Seated

When she said "Howdah do
Take a pew
You look divan"
I thought "This is sit"
But I was throne aside
When she decided to settle
For a pouffe
A sort of plinth charming
Who promised to support her
For the rest of her dais,
Next time I'll be more chairy.

The Tree of Love

Yew witch Hazel
It's plane
I'm sycamore poplar girls
And aspen alder time
On the beach
And pine to cedar day
When I maple to say
"Hazel lime yours,
Cumquat may."

A Musical Marriage

She would keep
Harping on about tidiness
Blowing her own trumpet
And drumming it into me
That I mustn't fiddle
With my hair
I think she was instrumental
In our divorce.

I Told Her

I told her no sensibleman
would take her dancing
in her bikini
So she went
With a little moron.

The Poet's Dilemma

Once upon a time I used
To mispell
To sometimes split infinitives
To get words of out order
To punctuate, —badly
To confused my tenses
To deem old words wondrous fair
to ignore capitals
To employ common or garden clichés
To miss the occasional out
To indulge in tautological repetitive
     statements
To exaggerate hundreds of times a day
And to repeat puns quite by chants
But worst of all I used
To forget to finish what I

CHAPS & MAPS

The Art of Biography
Is different from Geography
Geography is about maps,
But biography is about chaps.

And a versified biography is called a Clerihew. Here are a couple by E. Clerihew Bentley, the man who invented this particular form of poetry:

"I quite realized," said Columbus,
"That the earth was not a rhombus,
But I am a little annoyed
To find it an oblate spheroid."

"No, sir," said General Sherman,
"I did not enjoy the sermon;
Nor I didn't git any
Kick outer thc Litany."

My colleague Louis Phillips is a master of the art of versified biography. Here are his latest gems:

Robert DeNiro
Is a screen hero.
Only a slob
Would call him Bob.

Clara Bow
(You may know)
Made a hit
By emphasizing It.

Don Rickles
Tickles
By insulting folks.
Didn't you know that you stupid ox.

John D. Rockcfeller made a million
Oh, hell, he made a billion,
When he turned up soil,
Voila! Oil!

And for a poem that's a picture as well as a concise biography in verse, I don't think you could do better than this:

He rocked the boat,
Did Ezra Shrank.
These bubbles mark
        O
        O
        O
        O
        O
Where Ezra sank.

Here's another short poem that does two things at once. It tells a story and it looks good.

```
He went out one lovely night
     To call upon a miss,
And when he reached her resi-
     dence
                    this.
               like
          stairs
       up
    ran
He
Her papa met him at the door,
     He didn't see the miss.
He'll not go there again though
     —for
He
    ʇuǝʍ
         down
              sɹᴉɐʇs
              like
                   ˙sᴉɥʇ
```

POETIC INJUSTICE

Some of the most memorable short poems are also the most savage. Here are my six favorite ruthless rhymes. The first is by one of the world's greatest novelists, William Makepeace Thackeray, the author of *Vanity Fair*. The rest are the work of that most prolific (and impoverished) of poets, Anon.

Charlotte, having seen his body,
Borne before her on a shutter,
Like a well-conducted person
Went on cutting bread and butter.

Last night I slew my wife,
Stretched her on the parquet flooring;
I was loth to take her life,
But I had to stop her snoring.

O'er the rugged mountain's brow
Clara threw the twins she nursed,
And remarked, "I wonder now
Which will reach the bottom first?"

I had written to Aunt Maud,
   Who was on a trip abroad,
When I heard she'd died of cramp
   Just too late to save the stamp.

"There's been an accident!" they said,
"Your husband's cut in half; he's dead!"
"Indeed!" said Mrs. Brown. "Well, if you please
Would you send me the half that's got my keys."

Llewelyn Peter James Maguire,
Touched a live electric wire;
Back on his heels it sent him rocking—
His language (like the wire) was shocking.

POETIC PRINTOUT

The twenty-first century is almost upon us, and helping us toward it in fine style is the unique Kay Hines, inventor of the Sonnet Slot Machine, a device designed to satisfy the poet and the gambler in us all. According to Ms. Hines:

> This slot machine has, instead of the customary three or four windows, fourteen rows of five windows each. In each little window, instead of the usual images of lemons, bells, cherries, etc., a word or words appear, comprising an iambic foot for the classic fourteen-line pentameter sonnet. When a coin is inserted and the handle is pulled, all the words whirl around, stopping randomly to form one among potentially thousands of sonnets. There are possible combinations that yield the Petrarchan sonnet rhyme scheme (with variations between Italian and Sicilian sestet) and also the Shakespearean sonnet rhyme scheme. Achieving a perfect or near-perfect rhyme scheme returns the player either a jackpot or free plays. And every player receives a printout of the sonnet he has composed.

If you enjoy truly contemporary poetry you might like this. It was written by a computer.

How can the purple yeti be so red,
Or chestnuts, like a widgeon calmly groan?
No sheep is quite as crooked as a bed,
Though chickens ever try to hide a bone.
I grieve that greasy turnips slowly march:
Indeed, inflated is the icy pig:
For as the alligator strikes the larch,
So sighs the grazing goldfish for a wig.
Oh, has the pilchard argued with a top?
She never that the parsnip is too weird!
I tell thee that the wolf-man will not hop
And no man ever praised the convex beard.
Effulgent is the day when bishops turn:
So let not the doctor wake the urn!

It may read like nonsense (which it is) but the meter and the rhymes are spot on. It was produced by a computer fed with a long list of words, classified by parts of speech and numbers of syllables.

And if you don't like contemporary poetry, remember that the modern poet has a lot to contend with.

Inspiration and genius
Are not everything.
While Shakespeare wrote
The telephone didn't ring.

Shrewd Simon Short

In *The Joy of Lex* I presented some of the world's shortest (most terrible) tongue twisters, from "Greek grapes" to "Knapsack strap." In *More Joy of Lex* I am offering you the world's longest (most terrible) tongue twister: "The Saga of Shrewd Simon Short."

Try to read it out loud without making a single slip. I couldn't do it. Can you?

Shrewd Simon Short sewed shoes. Seventeen summers, speeding storms, spreading sunshine successively, saw Simon's small, shabby shop, still standing staunch, saw Simon's selfsame squeaking sign still swinging silently specifying:

Simon Short, Smithfield's sole surviving shoemaker. Shoes sewed soled superfinely.

Simon's spry, sedulous spouse, Sally Short, sewed shirts,

stitched sheets, stuffed sofas. Simon's six stout sons—Seth, Samuel, Stephen, Saul, Silas, Shadrach—sold sundries. Sober Seth sold sugar, spices; simple Sam sold saddles, stirrups, screws; sagacious Stephen sold silks, satins, shawls; skeptical Saul sold silver salvers; selfish Shadrach sold salves, shoestrings, soap, saws, skates; slack Silas sold Sally Short's stuffed sofas.

Some seven summers since, Simon's second son Samuel saw Sophia Sophronia Spriggs somewhere. Sweet, smart, sensible Sophia Sophronia Spriggs. Sam soon showed strong symptoms. Sam seldom stayed storing, selling saddles. Sam sighed sorrowfully, sought Sophia Sophronia's society, sung several serenades slyly. Simon stormed, scolded severely, said Sam seemed so silly singing such shameful, senseless songs. "Strange Sam should slight such splendid sales! Strutting spendthrift! Shattered-brained simpleton."

"Softly, softly, sire," said Sally. "Sam's smitten; Sam's spied some sweetheart."

"Sentimental schoolboy!" snarled Simon. "Smitten! Stop such stuff." Simon sent Sally's snuffbox spinning, seized Sally's scissors, smashed Sally's spectacles, scattering several spools. "Sneaking scoundrel! Sam's shocking silliness shall surcease!" Scowling, Simon stopped speaking, started swiftly shopward. Sally sighed sadly. Summoning Sam, she spoke sweet sympathy. "Sam," said she, "sire seems singularly snappy; so, solicit, sue, secure Sophronia speedily, Sam."

"So soon? So soon?" said Sam, standing stock-still.

"So soon, surely," said Sally smiling, "specially since sire shows such spirits."

So Sam, somewhat scared, sauntered slowly, shaking stupendously, Sam soliloquizes: "Sophia Sophronia Spriggs, Spriggs—Short—Sophia Sophronia Short—Samuel Short's spouse—sounds splendid! Suppose she should say—she shan't—she shan't!"

Soon Sam spied Sophia starching shirts, singing softly. Seeing Sam she stopped starching, saluting Sam smilingly. Sam stammered shockingly.

"Spl-spl-splendid summer season, Sophia."

"Selling saddles still, Sam?"

"Sar-sar-tin," said Sam, starting suddenly. "Season's somewhat sudorific," said Sam, steadily, staunching streaming sweat, shaking sensibly.

"Sartin," said Sophia, smiling significantly. "Sip some sweet sherbet, Sam." (Silence sixty seconds.)

"Sire shot sixty shelldrakes, Saturday," said Sophia.

"Sixty? Sho!" said Sam. (Silence seventy-seven seconds.)

"See sister Susan's sunflowers," said Sophia socially, silencing such stiff silence.

Sophia's sprightly sauciness stimulated Sam strangely: so Sam suddenly spoke sentimentally: "Sophia, Susan's sunflowers seem saying Samuel Short, Sophia Sophronia Spriggs, stroll serenely, seek some sequestered spot, some sylvan shade. Sparkling springs shall sing soul-stirring strains; sweet songsters shall silence secret sighings; super-angelic sylphs shall"— Sophia snickered; so Sam stopped.

"Sophia," said Sam solemnly.

"Sam," said Sophia.

"Sophia, stop smiling; Sam Short's sincere. Sam's seeking some sweet spouse, Sophia."

Sophia stood silent.

"Speak, Sophia, speak; such suspense speculates sorrow."

"Seek, sire, Sam, seek sire."

So Sam sought sire Spriggs; sire Spriggs said, "Sartin."

P.S. If a Hottentot tot taught a Hottentot tot to talk e'er the tot could totter, ought the Hottentot tot be taught to say aught, or naught, or what ought to be taught her?

If to hoot and to toot a Hottentot tot be taught by a Hottentot tutor, should the tutor get hot if the Hottentot tot hoot and toot at the Hottentot tutor?

RULES OF THE GAME

A great American once observed: "The Lord's Prayer has 56 words; at Gettysburg, Lincoln spoke only 268 long-remembered words; and we got a whole country goin' on the 1322 words in the Declaration of Independence. So how come it took the government 26,911 words to issue a regulation on the sale of cabbages?"

I don't know the answer to that one, but I do know that we would all write and speak better, clearer, and more understandable English if only we had learned the rules of the game. Which rules, you ask? These rules, says I.

1 Don't use no double negatives.

2 Make each pronoun agree with their antecedent.

3 Join clauses good, like a conjunction should.

4 About them sentence fragments.

5 When dangling watch your particles.

6 Verbs has to agree with their subjects.

7 Just between you and I, case is important too.

8 Don't write run-on sentences they are hard to read.

9 Don't use commas, which aren't necessary.

10 Try not to oversplit infinitives.

11 It is important to use your apostrophe's correctly.

12 Proofread your writing to if any words out.

13 Correct spelling is esential.

And here are two extra rules that, as a writer, I have found invaluable.

The Oxford rule. It's is not, it isn't ain't, and it's it's, not its, if you mean it is. If you don't, it's its. Then too, it's hers. It isn't her's. It isn't our's either. It's ours, and likewise yours and theirs.

Smith's writing rule. In composing, as a general rule, run your pen through every word you have written; you have no idea what vigor it will give your style.

Lifelaws

From Staten Island, New York, a reader recently wrote to me: "Dear Gyles, You seem to think you know a lot. Tell me, what is the meaning of life?"

Well, dear reader, I don't like admitting this—and you may find it hard to believe—but I don't know nothing about the Meaning of Life. At the same time, I hate disappointing anyone; so, just for the fun of it, I have gathered together my favorite Lifelaws: the rules, observations, and maxims that may not explain all the mysteries of life on this planet but at least help make it a whole lot more bearable. Here they are:

Blick's Rule of Life. You have two chances, slim and non-existent.

Brenne's Laws of Life. (1) You never get it where you want it. (2) If you think it's tough now, just wait.

Gandhi's Observation. There is more to life than increasing its speed.

Hovanick's Wait-till-Tomorrow Principle. Today is the last day of the first part of your life.

Howe's Verities. (1) When you're in trouble, people who call to sympathize are really looking for the particulars. (2) When in doubt in society, shake hands. (3) Everyone hates a martyr; it's no wonder martyrs are burned at the stake. (4) A good many of your tragedies probably look like comedies to others. (5) Put cream and sugar on a fly, and it tastes very much like a black raspberry. (6) Families with babies and families without babies are sorry for each other. (7) Where the guests at a gathering are acquainted, they eat 20 percent more than they otherwise would.

Freud's Observation. Shunning women, drink, gambling, smoking, and eating will not make one live longer; it will only seem like it.

Lee's Law. Mother said there would be days like this, but she never said there would be so many.

Lichtenberg's Insights. (1) If life were "just a bowl of cherries" . . . we would soon die of a deficiency disease. (2) We can never get to the Promised Land, for if we did, it would no longer be the Promised Land. (3) We say that the plough made civilization, but for that matter, so did manure. (4) The planning laws in most American neighborhoods would not *permit* the construction of a Parthenon.

Lucy's Law. The alternative to getting old is depressing.

Paige's Six Rules of Life (guaranteed to bring anyone to a happy old age.) (1) Avoid fried foods that angry up the blood. (2) If your stomach antagonizes you, pacify it with cool thoughts. (3) Keep the juices flowing by jangling around gently as you move. (4) Go very lightly on the vices, such as carrying on in society, as the social ramble ain't restful. (5) Avoid running at all times. (6) Don't look back, something might be gaining on you.

Quality-of-Life Constant. Every time in your life when you think you are about to be able to make both ends meet, somebody moves the ends.

Schwartz's True View of Life. Don't look for your real success until you're past fifty. It takes that long to get over the distractions of sex.

Schwartz's Maxim. Live every day as if it were your last . . . and some day you'll be right.

SIGNS OF MATURITY

Or: How to know you are growing older.

1 Everything hurts, and what doesn't hurt doesn't work.

2 The gleam in your eye is from the sun hitting your bifocals.

3 You feel like the night before, and you haven't been anywhere.

4 Your little black book contains only names ending in M.D.

5 You get winded playing chess.

6 Your children begin to look middle aged.

7 A dripping faucet causes an uncontrollable bladder urge.

8 You join a health club and don't go.

9 You know all the answers, but nobody asks you the questions.

10 You look forward to a dull evening.

11 You turn out the lights for economic rather than romantic reasons.

12 You sit in a rocking chair and can't get it going.

13 Your knees buckle but your belt won't.

14 Your back goes out more than you do.

15 The little gray-haired lady you help across the street is your wife.

16 You have too much room in the house and not enough in the medicine cabinet.

17 You sink your teeth into a steak, and they stay there.

QUOTE UNQUOTE

Messing about in quotes is one of my favorite pastimes, and
many of my favorite quotes have to do with words and language. Of my favorites the twenty-five that follow are my most
favorite. (*Favorite*, incidentally, is one of my favorite words. I
hope you don't think I overuse it. I try to avoid clichés like the
plague.)

> Man is a creature who lives not upon bread alone, but prin-
> cipally by catchwords. (ROBERT LOUIS STEVENSON)

> Man does not live by words alone, despite the fact that some-
> times he has to eat them. (ADLAI STEVENSON)

> Words, in their primary or immediate signification, stand for
> nothing but the ideas in the mind of him who uses them.
> (JOHN LOCKE)

If language be not in accordance with the truth of things, affairs cannot be carried on to success. (CONFUCIUS)

If a people have no word for something, either it does not matter to them or it matters too much to talk about it. (EDGAR Z. FRIEDENBERG)

Words should be an intense pleasure just as leather should be to a shoemaker. (EVELYN WAUGH)

Neither is a dictionary a bad book to read. There is no cant in it, no excess of explanation, and it is full of suggestion—the raw material of possible poems and histories. (RALPH WALDO EMERSON)

Dictionaries are like watches: the worst is better than none, and the best cannot be expected to go quite true. (SAMUEL JOHNSON)

When I feel inclined to read poetry I take down my dictionary. The poetry of words is quite as beautiful as that of sentences. (OLIVER WENDELL HOLMES, SR.)

The trouble with the dictionary is that you have to know how a word is spelled before you can look it up to see how it is spelled. (WILL CUPPY)

Many people would be more truthful were it not for their uncontrollable desire to talk. (EDWARD WATSON HOWE)

Talkers are no good doers. (WILLIAM SHAKESPEARE)

The habit of common and continuous speech is a symptom of mental deficiency. It proceeds from not knowing what is going on in other people's minds. (WALTER BAGEHOT)

Learned conversation is either the affectation of the ignorant or the profession of the mentally unemployed. (OSCAR WILDE)

The art of conversation is the art of hearing as well as of being heard. (WILLIAM HAZLITT)

It usually takes more than three weeks to prepare a good impromptu speech. (MARK TWAIN)

An unusual word should be shunned as a ship would shun a reef. (JULIUS CAESAR)

Short words are best and the old words when short are best of all. (WINSTON CHURCHILL)

Actions lie louder than words. (CAROLYN WELLS)

The Romans would never have found time to conquer the world if they had been obliged first to learn Latin. (HEINRICH HEINE)

A man of words and not deeds is like a garden full of weeds. (ENGLISH PROVERB)

A fine quotation is a diamond on the finger of a man of wit, and a pebble in the hand of a fool. (JOSEPH ROUX)

A short saying oft contains much wisdom. (SOPHOCLES)

I hate quotations. Tell me what you know. (RALPH WALDO EMERSON)

WHAT I KNOW

I know I love quotations, especially ones that make you smile—and think, like these:

If the art of conversation stood a little higher, we would have a lower birthrate. (STANISLAW LEC)

Bureaucracy is based on a willingness either to pass the buck or spend it. (MRS. HENRY J. SERWAT)

It's hard to know exactly when one generation ends and the next one begins. But it's somewhere around nine o'clock at night. (CHARLES RUFFING)

My interest is in the future, because I am going to spend the rest of my life there. (CHARLES KETTERING)

EROS: spelled backwards gives you an idea of how it affects beginners. (ANONYMOUS)

To double your salary, Xerox your paycheck. (PAT O'HAIRE)

If soldiers were asked to do in battle what the average motorist does on weekends for fun, the officer in charge would be court-martialed for brutality. (MALCOLM MUGGERIDGE)

When in doubt, tell the truth. (MARK TWAIN)

A kiss that speaks volumes is seldom a first edition. (CLARE WHITING)

Whenever you hear the word *save*, it is usually the beginning of an advertisement designed to make you spend money. (RENÉE PIERRE-GOSSET)

If God had meant people to go nude, they would have been born that way. (ad in THE VILLAGE VOICE)

If God had meant us to go metric, why did he give Christ twelve apostles? (GYLES BRANDRETH)

PRAY TIME

How long (O Lord) will it be, I wonder, before our prayers have been translated into the language of our times? The jargoneers are working on the Psalms already: "The Lord and I are in a shepherd/sheep situation and I am in a position of negative need . . ."

With a little luck—and possibly some divine intervention—the language of prayer may remain sacred for a few years yet.

It's the *language* of prayer that is so compelling, even if some of the *sentiments* expressed are not so worthy.

THE CAPITOL HILL PRAYER

Yea, though I graze in pastures with jackasses,
I pray that I may not bray like one.

THE BIGOT'S PRAYER

Grant, O God, that we may always be right, for Thou knowest
we will never change our minds.

THE FISHERMAN'S PRAYER

Give me, O Lord, to catch a fish
    So large that even I,
In boasting of it afterwards,
    Shall have no need to lie.

THE PRAGMATIST'S PRAYER

Searcher of souls, You who in heaven abide,
To whom the secrets of all hearts are open,
Though I do lie to all the world beside,
From me to these no falsehoods shall be spoken.
Cleanse me not, Lord, I say, from secret sin
But from those faults which he who runs can see.
'Tis these that torture me, O Lord, begin
With these and let the hidden vices be;
If You must cleanse these too, at any rate
Deal with the seen sins first, 'tis only reason,
They being so gross, to let the others wait
The leisure of some more convenient season;
    And cleanse not all even then, leave me a few,
    I would not be—not quite—so pure as You.

THE PRAYER OF THE GYPSY MODORAN

Sweet little God, I beseech thee to grant me everything I ask,
because thou art beautiful, high, and mighty.

    If thou lettest me steal a loaf, brandy, a hen, a goose, a pig,
or a horse, I will give thee a big candle.

    If I have stolen anything, and the Gentiles enter my tent to
discover the stolen property and find nothing, I will give thee
two big candles.

If the officer of the law enter my tent and, having searched it and found nothing, depart in peace, I will give thee three big candles.

Because thou art my sweet little golden God.

PRAYER OF A POOR PEDESTRIAN

O God, who filled all heaven with stars
And then all earth with motorcars,
    Make room within thy cosmic plan
    For me, a poor pedestrian.

Spread Thou before me, I entreat,
A threadlike pathway for my feet;
    And do Thou watch me lest I stray
    From this, Thy strait and narrow way.

Give me an ear alert, acute,
For each swift car's peremptory hoot:
    Teach me to judge its headlong pace
    And dodge it with a nimble grace.

When drivers' looks and words are black,
Restrain me, Lord, from answering back:
    O bless me with a nature meek
    To bear with smiles each narrow squeak.

And if one day Thy watchful eye
Should be withdrawn, and I should die,
    One boon I crave, upon my knees:
    Exonerate the driver, please.

THE VENDOR'S PRAYER

On Sunday, Lord, a Mrs. Drew
Is coming here the house to view,
    Which is, of course, for sale.
Grant Thou, O Lord, that she forbear
From standing long upon the stair
    That is, alas! too frail.

O do not let her hand draw back
The curtain and reveal the crack
    Along the windowpane!
O guide her as she comes and goes,
So that no smell assails her nose
    From the adjacent drain.

Let her not see the neighboring slum
As she approaches. May she come
    Along the better road,
And grant that she may, in a trice,
Agree to the inflated price
    We ask for our abode.

And grant, O Lord, to us who plead,
These favors that we may succeed
    In what we now devise,
And through thine all-embracing love
Be made eternal tenants of
    Thy mansion in the skies.

THE HUSBAND'S PRAYER

Lord, on whom all love depends,
Let me make and keep good friends:
Bless me, also, with the patience
To endure my wife's relations.

THE BARGAINING PRAYER

Lord, give us grace, for if Thou give us not grace, we shall not give Thee glory; and who will win by that, Lord?

Recently a prayer—albeit not a very poetic one—managed to make legal history when it was quoted in the trial of a man accused of starting a forest fire in British Columbia.

The accused claimed that what he had said was inadmissible as evidence because it formed part of a "private conversation" he was having with God. The judge ruled that it was not possible to have a genuine conversation with God since He/She was not legally a person.

Consequently the man's prayer was admitted as evidence and established as proof of his guilt. This was the unfortunate prayer: "Oh God, please let me get away with it, just this once."

O
H NO IT'S NOT!

The world of words is full of surprises. You might think that a
barguest is a guest in a bar, but, oh no, it's not. It's a ghost or a
goblin, often shaped like a large dog. And if you need further
proof that words aren't always what they seem, here it is:

> *Bedrape* is not rape occurring in a bed; but is an intensive form
> of the verb *drape*.

> *Bedrug* is not a bedspread; but is an intensive form of the verb
> *drug*.

> *Carlot* is not a place for parking or displaying cars; but is an
> obsolete term for a book.

> *Deadlily* is not a dead lily; but is an adverb meaning "in a deadly
> manner."

> *Forestation* is not a station or outpost at a frontier; but is the
> establishment of a forest.

Forestress is not a female forester; but is a verb meaning "to place stress on the first part of a word."

Interminable is not an adjective meaning "to penetrate with mines"; but is an adjective meaning "long-lasting."

Intermine is not a verb meaning "to last for a long time"; but is a verb meaning "to penetrate with mines."

Negrocop is not a black policeman; but is a type of stork, also called the jabiru.

Nunlet is not a small nun; but is a small South American bird.

Racemate is not a member of the same race; but is a chemical salt of racemic acid.

Redial is not a verb meaning "to dial again"; but is an adjective meaning "relating to redia, a type of larva."

Restable is not a verb meaning "to stable again"; but is an adjective meaning "able to rest."

Sealess is not a female seal; but is an adjective meaning "without a sea."

Tonite is not only a slang spelling of *tonight;* but is also a blasting explosive.

Townsite is not a mineral named after someone named Towns; but is the site of a town.

Wellsite is not the site of a well; but is a mineral named after someone named Wells.

N EOLOGISTS AT WORK

In the 1960s, 70s, and 80s, the neologists have been hard at work, creating brand-new words for a brave new world. Here are thirty long ones:

antientertainment

biodeterioration

biogeocoenology

bourgeoisification

comprehensivization

containershipping

counterdemonstrator

cross-subsidization

dendroclimatologist

electrogasdynamic

embourgeoisification

encephalomyocarditis

Finlandization

hyperlipoproteinemia

intergenerational

Malaysianization

Manhattanization

megahallucinogen

microearthquake

mini-black-hole

neuropharmacological
nucleocosmochronology
pachycephalosaurian
psychedelicatessen
psychobiographical

suggestopaedia
tephrochronological
transhistorical
undercharacterization
Washingtonologist

And here are thirty phrases of our time, and each one has made its way into the dictionary during the final third of the twentieth century:

animal lib
big enchilada
brown power
clockwork orange
double nickel
empty nest syndrome
floppy disk
game plan
home computer
hot pants
incomes policy
Jesus freak
junk food
kinky boot
last hurrah

male chauvinist piggery
meter maid
neutron bomb
oil spill
phone phreakdom
quick and dirty
reverse discrimination
Saturday night special
tadpole galaxy
urban sprawl
value-added tax
Wankel engine
X-rated
youth culture
zero population growth

Barnhart language

A Dictionary of New English and The Second Barnhart Dictionary of New English, both by Clarence Barnhart, Robert Barnhart, and Sol Steinmetz, were published in 1973 and 1980, respectively, and they feature words, initials, phrases, abbreviations, acronyms, and meanings that have entered the vocabulary of the English language in very recent years.

A number of the entries are of words relating to words. Here are thirty:

acrolet	The dialect that has the most prestige among the speakers of a language.
AmeroEnglish	American English.
bookaholic	A person addicted to books.
businesspeak	Commercial jargon.
dead letter box	A place for depositing secret messages.
educationese	Jargon used by people associated with education.
encryption	The act of putting information into a code.
English English	English as spoken in England.
Englishment	An English version of a foreign work.
exonym	Any of the names given in different countries or languages to the same geographical feature.
expletive deleted	An expression indicating the omission from print of an obscene word or phrase.
factoid	A published statement taken to be a fact by virture of its appearance in print.
familygram	A brief radio message transmitted by relatives to a sailor at sea.
francisize	To cause to change to the French language.
francophonic	French-speaking.
franglification	The introduction of English words and expressions into French.
Fringlish	English containing French words and expressions.
Hinglish	A blend of Hindi and English spoken in India.
Japlish	A blend of Japanese and English spoken in Japan.
jargonaut	A person who uses jargon excessively.
Jonah word	Any word that a chronic stutterer has difficulty uttering in ordinary conversation.

lansign	A word, character, or sound that represents a thing or idea.
pangram	A sentence made up to include all the letters of the alphabet.
psychobabble	Psychological jargon.
semiliterate	A person barely able to read and write.
single-entendre	A word, expression, or statement with an unmistakable and often indelicate meaning.
Spanglish	A blend of Spanish and English spoken in parts of the western United States and Latin America.
whydunit	A mystery novel that deals primarily with the motivation for the crime.
wordaholic	A word addict.
Yinglish	English containing many Yiddish words and expressions.

TIMELY NEOLOGISMS

For well over four decades now, *Time* magazine has been introducing words to the English language.

Tycoon, kudos, pundit, and *socialite* all gained currency from their use in *Time*. The magazine was the first to put *Op* in *Op Art,* and it led the way in popularizing scores of new words, from *G.I.* to *A-bomb,* from *beatnik* to *McCarthyism,* and from *Kremlinologist* to *Sinologist.* Of course *Time* has had its share of failures. It tried hard with *cinemactor, cinemactress,* and *cinemogul,* but none of them caught on.

Here are some of *Time*'s new words from the sixties and seventies. The magazine created many of the words and popularized the others. What all the words have in common is that when *Time* was first published none of them existed.

amorific (1975)	apocalypticians (1972)
anti-opera (1968)	audioanimatronically (1973)
anti-star (1969)	Beatledammerung (1971)

bewilderness (1973)
biographoid (1973)
blaxploitation (1974)
buffdom (1974)
Californicated (1971)
Carterphobia (1976)
cavepersons (1976)
chillout (1973)
counterklutzical (1976)
crediholics (1977)
culturecrats (1970)
Disneyfication (1977)
eco-activists (1969)
ejaculatorium (1972)
girlcott (1970)
growthmania (1977)
heightism (1971)
hippophile (1970)
horsepersons (1976)
jivernacular (1975)
lumpengrandiosity (1974)
mailgrams (1977)
Maocidal (1977)
mathemagician (1977)
mazemania (1975)
megabuckers (1977)
megadisaster (1976)
Msapprehension (1972)
Msogamy (1971)
occultivated (1975)
oligosyllabic (1971)
orgasmatron (1975)
outcumbent (1976)

paperkrieg (1973)
parafictions (1977)
petroglitter (1975)
petropolitics (1973)
phallocrat (1977)
philodendrophiles (1974)
plantochondriacs (1974)
polycopulative (1971)
prognosticide (1974)
radicalesbians (1970)
roadies (1973)
schleprechaun (1972)
sci-fireworks (1976)
sexscraper (1970)
sociohysteric (1973)
space-bopper (1975)
superbug (1977)
supercrooner (1973)
superpregnancy (1973)
superscapegoat (1973)
systemaniac (1977)
televangelist (1973)
UFOria (1976)
underworldly (1970)
unsavvy (1976)
urbanscape (1975)
verballistics (1972)
vestphobe (1974)
watch-birds (1971)
womandarin (1972)
wommanequin (1971)
womlibby (1973)

MEDICINEOLOGY

Of course, living in the 1980s we all face certain health hazards. Fortunately, the neologists among the medics have found appropriate names for the ailments of our times. These ten were noted by *The New England Journal of Medicine:*

Rubik Cuber's Tendonitis

Yo-Yoers Finger

Jogger's Nipple

Cyclist's Pudendum

Dog Walker's Elbow

Space Invader's Wrist

Unicyclist's Sciatica

Jeans Folliculitis

Flautist's Neuropathy

Urban Cowboy's Rhabdomyolisis (A muscular pain caused by riding mechanical bucking broncos in amusement arcades.)

M

Y KIND OF TOWN

In *Webster's Third New International Dictionary*, the noun *Chicago* is defined as a method of playing contract bridge in sets of four deals rather than rubbers. The dictionary also indicates that *Chicago* is a synonym for *Michigan*, a type of card game. I wonder just how many people know that *Chicago* and *Michigan* are one and the same thing?

It's surprising how many city names happen to have alternative meanings. Take these for a start:

Amarillo	A Venezuelan tree.
Atlanta	A genus of molluscs.
Austin	Relating to St. Augustus.
Baltimore	A butterfly.
Boston	A waltz.

Buffalo	To bewilder.
Charlotte	A dessert.
Cincinnati	A wild-card poker game.
Dearborn	A light four-wheeled carriage.
Denver	Battleship gray, a color.
Fresno	A modified drag scraper, an earth digging device.
Long Beach	A light yellowish brown color.
Milwaukee	A variety of apple.
Montgomery	An Asian Indian breed of dairy cattle.
Phoenix	A legendary bird.
Springfield	A U.S. army rifle.
Toledo	A sword.
Wichita	An Indian people.
Worcester	A type of china or porcelain.
Yonkers	Young men.

Some state names have unexpected alternative meanings too. Look at these:

Alabama	A genus of moths.
Alaska	A mixed yarn.
Arkansas	A type of apple.
Delaware	One of a breed of fowls.
Florida	A large yellow peach.
Georgia	A feminine proper name.
Idaho	A potato.
Indiana	A vivid red color.
Kansas	An adjective used to refer to the second glacial stage during the glacial epoch in North America.
Maine	To lower a sail.
Maryland	Tobacco.
Michigan	A card game.
Minnesota	A breed of swine.
Mississippi	A game resembling bagatelle.

Montana	A sheep.
Nevada	Pseudonymous surname of Emma Wixom, an American singer.
New Hampshire	A fowl.
Oklahoma	A form of gin rummy.
Oregon	A ship.
Texas	The narrow topmost story of a grain elevator.

CHICAGO

Everyone is familiar with the name Chicago, but the way we spell it today isn't how it has always been spelled. In fact there is probably no other city in the United States whose name over the years has been spelled in so many different ways. *Chicago* is a word of Indian origin, supposedly meaning "garlic," "wild onion," and "pskunk."

Can you guess how many known alternative spellings for *Chicago* there have been over the past three hundred years?

(See Answers.)

DING DONG IN TEXAS

The United States boasts some remarkable place names. I've made a list of my favorites and I plan to go visit most of them one day. As names, they may seem incredible, but I promise that you'll find every one of them on the map.

Aaat's Bay	(Alaska)
Bad Axe	(Michigan)
Battiest	(Oklahoma)
Bald Knob	(Arkansas)
Bird in Hand	(Pennsylvania)
Blue Earth	(Minnesota)
Broken Bow	(Nebraska)

Bug	(Kentucky)
Cut Off	(Louisiana)
Cut and Shoot	(Texas)
Ding Dong	(Texas)
D'Lo	(Mississippi)
E	(Maine)
Eek	(Alaska)
Eighty Eight	(Kentucky)
Embarrass	(Wisconsin)
Enigma	(Georgia)
Flying H	(New Mexico)
Gravel Switch	(Kentucky)
Gu Vo	(Arizona)
Hi Hat	(Kentucky)
Horse Thief	(Arizona)
Hungry Horse	(Montana)
Intercourse	(Pennsylvania)
Jackass Flats	(Nevada)
King of Prussia	(Pennsylvania)
Kupk	(Arizona)
Left Hand	(West Virginia)
Marrowbone	(Kentucky)
Mexican Hat	(Utah)
Nameless	(Kentucky)
Novelty	(Ohio)
Only	(Tennessee)
Plain Dealing	(Louisiana)
Sikul Himatk	(Arizona)
Sivili Chuchg	(Arizona)
Slap Out	(Illinois)
Smoky Ordinary	(Virginia)
Social Circle	(Georgia)
Sweet Gum Head	(Louisiana)
Tobacco	(Kentucky)

Truth or Consequences	(New Mexico)
Uncle Same	(Louisiana)
Wawk Hudunk	(Arizona)
What Cheer	(Iowa)
Why	(Arizona)
Whynot	(Mississippi)
Wounded Knee	(South Dakota)
Yum Yum	(Tennessee)
Zzyzx Springs	(California)

Wyoming in delaware

My good friend Darryl Francis, committed verbivore and student of geography, has discovered that there are two hundred cities, towns, and communities in the United States that have names that happen also to be the names of states. For example, there is a town called *Oregon* in Holt County, Missouri, and a *Maine* in Davie County, North Carolina.

There is even a *New Hampshire* in Auglaize County, Ohio, and a *West Virginia* in St. Louis County, Minnesota.

Here are twenty-six of the places Darryl discovered, arranged in an elegant chain of town and state names:

Wyoming is in Kent County, Delaware.

Delaware is in Southampton County, Virginia.

Virginia is in Kitsap County, Washington.

Washington is in Knox County, Maine.

Maine is in Coconino County, Arizona.

Arizona is in Burt County, Nebraska.

Nebraska is in Jennings County, Indiana.

Indiana is in Indiana County, Pennsylvania.

Pennsylvania is in Mobile County, Alabama.

Alabama is in Genesee County, New York.

New York is in Santa Rosa County, Florida.

Florida is in Houghton County, Michigan.

Michigan is in Osage County, Kansas.

Kansas is in Seneca County, Ohio.

Ohio is in Gunnison County, Colorado.

Colorado is in South Central District, Alaska.

Alaska is in Mineral County, West Virginia.

West Virginia is in St. Louis County, Minnesota.

Minnesota is in Colquitt County, Georgia.

Georgia is in Lamar County, Texas.

Texas is in Baltimore County, Maryland.

Maryland is in East Baton Rouge County, Louisiana.

Louisiana is in Pike County, Missouri.

Missouri is in Brown County, Illinois.

Illinois is in Sequoyah County, Oklahoma.

Oklahoma is in Daviess County, Kentucky.

I'M ACHING FOR MICHIGAN

Rearrange the letters in *Colorado,* and you can make *coal odor* or *cool road*. Rearrange the letters in the names of two dozen other states, and you get a curious collection of alternative words, names, and places.

Alaska	*Akalas* are certain shrubs that bear large red edible fruits and come from the Hawaiian Islands.
Arizona	*Arzonia* is a girl's given name; *Azorian* is a native of the Azores Islands; *Zonaria* is a group of mammals including the carnivores and certain ungulates.
Arkansas	*Sankara's* is the possessive or genitive form of Sankara, a famous Hindu philosopher who flourished around A.D. 800. *Sanskara* is a Hindu ceremony that purifies the taint of sin contracted in the womb.
California	*African oil* is a type of palm oil yielded by a tall palm tree, the African oil palm.

Delaware	*Aleeward* is toward the sheltered side; *Weardale* is a district of the town of Durham in England.
Florida	*Forlaid* is the past tense of *forlay*, to hinder or obstruct.
Idaho	*Adhoi* is a town in India, west of Ahmedabad, along the Tropic of Cancer.
Illinois	*Illision* is the act of dashing or striking against something.
Indiana	*Anidian* is an adjective meaning "formless," or "without shape."
Iowa	*Aiwo* is one of the fourteen regions of Nauru Island, in the Pacific; *Awio* Bay is on the southern coast of New Britain, in New Guinea.
Kansas	*Asansk* is a town northeast of Krasnoyarsk, in west central Siberia; *Kassan* is a town southwest of Samarkand in Uzbekistan; *Nassak* is the name of a world-famous diamond. (Note that *KASSAN* and *NASSAK* are reversals of each other.)
Maine	*Amine* is a type of organic compound; *Meina* is a town in Italy; *Menai* Strait is in Wales; *Namie* is a town in Japan.
Maryland	*Marlandy* Hill is a 1,230-foot-high hill near the western coast of Australia.
Minnesota	*Mainstone* is a town in Shropshire, England; *Mannitose* is a type of sugar; *Nominates* simply means "designates."
Montana	*Manaton* is a town in Devonshire, England.
Nebraska	*Bankeras* are stone curlews of Santo Domingo; *Branksea* is an ecclesiastical district in southeast Devonshire, England.
Nevada	*Adaven* is a community in Nye County, Nevada. (Note that this is *Nevada* spelled backwards.) *Venada* is another name for a pudu, a type of deer.
New York	*Ywroken* is an old form of the past participle of the verb *wreak*, now occuped by *wrought*.

Ohio	*Hooi* is the sound made by the wind whistling around a corner or through a keyhole.
Oregon	*Orgone* is a vital energy held to pervade nature and to be accumulable, in a specially designed box, for use by humans; *oronge* is an old spelling of *orange*.
Texas	*Sexta* is a feminine first name; *taxes* is the plural of *tax*.
Utah	*Ahut* is a fourteenth-century variant spelling of *aught; haut* is an old word for *height; thau* is the twenty-third letter of the Hebrew alphabet, also called *tav* and *taw*.
Virginia	*Irvingia* is a genus of tree.
Washington	*Nowanights* is the nighttime equivalent of *nowadays*.

Teen sense in Tennessee

Take these twenty words and rearrange the letters in each word to form the names of twenty American cities.

1	annotations	11	Havanans
2	brogan	12	hounds
3	capers	13	long leases
4	caption	14	meals
5	counts	15	nerved
6	diagnose	16	ordeal
7	domains	17	Nero
8	dottier	18	salvages
9	emendator	19	tooled
10	grained	20	wine cellars

(See Answers.)

LARGESSE IS A CAPITAL S

These aren't bona fide boners. They are bogus bloopers made up by those who know better and are simply designed to raise a smile.

1 *Largesse* is a capital S.

2 A male escort is known as a *mandate*.

3 *Maritime affairs* refer to what happens on wedding days.

4 Judges always appear in a *lawsuit*.

5 *Cereal* is an adjective that describes the painting style of Salvador Dali.

6 A *bombard* is a lousy poet.

7 A *locomotion* is a faint noise.

8 A *handicap* is a ready hat.

9 Your ex-spouse is known as a *stalemate*.

10 A *shamrock* is a fake diamond.

These ones are the real thing: genuine mistakes committed by the innocent in schools and colleges around the English-speaking world.

1 Garibaldi designed the Statue of Liberty.

2 Flaura and Fauna were the original Siamese twins.

3 *A priori* means first come first served.

4 Daniel Boone was born in a log cabin he built himself.

5 *Iran* is the Moslem Bible.

6 *Bambi* is a book about Babe Ruth.

7 The eastern part of Asia is called Euthenasia.

8 The Metropolitan area of New York is the district near the Metropolitan Opera House.

9 The American people have the right to partition Congress without going to jail.

10 *Mata Hari* means suicide in Japanese.

11 Bisquit Tortoni is the man who discovered radio.

12 Poetic license is the license you need so that you can sell poetry.

13 Davy Jones was a famous train engineer.

14 Plenipotentiary is a place where foreign prisoners are kept.

15 The Merchant of Venice was a famous Italian who bought and sold canal boats.

16 Electric volts are named after Voltaire who discovered electricity.

17 When a woman has many husbands she is called a Pollyana.

18 A stowaway is the man with the biggest appetite on the ship.

19 Latin Quarter is a French twenty-five-cent piece.

20 The Angelus is the home of the angels up in the sky.

Dr. Alan Adell, Professor of Semantics at the University of Michigan in Ann Arbor, has recently completed a study of high-school vocabularies and come to the conclusion that children are much more likely to misunderstand a word if they hear it spoken than if they see it written. The students were each asked to define one hundred words given to them orally/aurally. These are some of the ones they got wrong.

adamant	Pertaining to original sin.
aerie	Opposite of bold.
agnostics	Behavior of sound.
allegro	Chorus line.
amidst	Thick fog.
anthem	Quite good-looking.
antibody	Diet.
antimony	Money inherited from an aunt.
appendix	Part of a book with little use.
asperity	Drug from which aspirins are made.
aviary	Pilots' dormitory.
bibliography	Holy geography.
blizzard	Inside of a chicken.
buttress	Nanny goat.
caboose	Indian baby.
centimeter	Insect with one hundred legs.
chinchilla	Icepack for lower half of the face.
concubine	Merger of several businesses.
conservation	Table talk.
counterspy	Store detective.
dermatology	Study of derms.
deciduous	Able to make up one's mind.
diatribe	Food for the whole clan.
diva	Swimming champion.
doggerell	Little dog.
effusive	Able to be merged.
epitaph	Short, sarcastic poem.
equestrian	Person living on the equator.
executive	Man who puts others to death.
finesse	Female fish.

firecracker	Hot biscuit.
genealogy	Allergic to denim.
gubernatorial	To do with peanuts.
gullible	To do with sea birds.
hackneyed	Opposite of knock-kneed.
hysterics	Letters in sloping type.
ingenious	Not very smart.
incommode	Engaged, occupied.
journeyman	Traveling man.
kilocycle	Dangerous two-wheeler.
liter	Group of puppies.
longevity	Being very tall.
long-winded	In good physical condition.
nitrate	Off-peak charges.
optimists	Doctors that treat your eyes.
pedigree	Teacher in college.
pemmican	Large bird with large bill.
physics	Different shapes of the human body.
pigamist	Man with more than one wife.
polyglot	More than one glot.
polygon	Another name for a Mormon.
preface	Before applying makeup.
reefs	Objects placed on coffins.
sabbatical year	Year with fifty-three Sundays.
semiquaver	Half afraid.
stalemate	Husband or wife no longer interesting.
telepathy	Code invented by Morse.
tenet	Group of ten singers.
typographer	Student and drawer of maps.
vicar	Masculine form of *vixen*.

K.O. OK?

Told by a lady from Boston that her ancestors had sailed on the *Mayflower*, Will Rogers calmly replied that his ancestors had been waiting on the beach to meet them.

When you are bandying words with a true wit like Will Rogers, you'd better watch out. With his kind, you can find yourself K.O.'d before you realize the fight's begun.

For years now I have been collecting accounts of wits at work—and the more wicked and waspish they are being in their wittiness the happier I am. From your ringside seat you should be able to relax and enjoy these stories. After all, you can afford to. You're not one of the victims.

Ensnared by a fellow Bostonian who had pretensions to great piety, Mark Twain suffered the man for several minutes while he recounted his latest works of charity, concluding with the solemn pronouncement that his greatest ambition was to travel to the Holy Land and recite the Ten Commandments on Mt. Sinai before he died.

"Really," said Twain, "and why not stay here in Boston and keep them?"

Only a few years before his death, Mozart was visited by a young composer who wanted to know how to write a symphony.

"You're very young," the great man told him. "Shouldn't you start by composing ballads?"

"But you were composing symphonies when you were only ten."

"I know," said Mozart, "but I didn't have to ask how."

Henry Clay was famous for his intolerance of the loquacious. Sitting in the Senate one day, he was forced to listen to one of the most prolix members of the House, who insisted on punctuating his speech with erudite references and rhetorical flourishes. Eventually Clay got to his feet and complained to the Speaker about the man.

"You, sir, speak for the present generation," said the aggrieved orator. "But I speak for posterity."

"Yes," replied Clay, "and you seem resolved to speak until the arrival of your audience."

William Howard Taft and Chauncey Depew were both invited as guests of honor to an important Washington dinner before Taft was elected to the White House. During the meal they indulged in a little familiar sparring:

"I hope, if it's a girl, Mr. Taft will name it for his charming wife," said Depew with an eye on Taft's prodigious girth.

"If it is a girl, I shall, of course, name it for my lovely helpmate of many years," replied Taft. "And if it's a boy, I shall claim the father's prerogative and name it Junior. But, if, as I suspect, it is only a bag of wind, I shall name it Chauncey Depew."

During his term as Governor of New Jersey, Woodrow Wilson took a phone call informing him of the sudden death of one of his great friends, who represented the State in Congress. While he was still sitting at his desk, stunned by the news, the phone rang again. This time it was another New Jersey politician who had also heard the sad news but who wanted to capitalize on the sudden announcement. Could he take the deceased senator's place?

"Well, you may quote me as saying that's perfectly agreeable to me if it's agreeable to the undertaker," Wilson told him.

As a young man Heywood Broun was sent to interview a very haughty member of Congress on a very controversial subject.

"I have nothing to say, young man," said the Congressman before Broun had even opened his notebook.

"I know," Broun told him. "Now, shall we get on with the interview?"

"Mr. President, you must give me a colonel's commission for my son," a pushy mother informed Lincoln. "Sir, I demand it, not as a favor, but as a right. Sir, my grandfather fought at Lexington. Sir, my uncle was the only man who did not run away at Bladensburg. Sir, my father fought at New Orleans, and my husband was killed at Monterey."

"I guess, madam, your family has done enough for the country," Lincoln told her. "I think the time has come to give somebody else a chance."

Trying to capture the right expression from a very talkative and fidgety subject, Max Liebermann, the famous Berlin artist, silenced the woman with the comment:

"One more word out of you and I'll paint you as you are."

Once, when William McNeill Whistler was in France and dining in a fashionable restaurant, he extended the hand of kindness and had it bitten. At the table next to him sat an Englishman who was experiencing some difficulty in placing an order in French.

"May I help you?" enquired Whistler politely, only to receive a curt rebuff to the effect that the man could manage on his own.

"I fancied contrary just now," replied Whistler, "when I heard you desire the waiter to bring you a pair of stairs."

Asked her opinion of a fellow artiste, the legendary Sarah Bernhardt replied:

"She's a wonderful actress from the waist down."

In the same (varicose) vein, Bette Davis is said to have remarked once of a Hollywood starlet: "There goes the good time that's had by all."

An amateur critic who buttonholed George S. Kaufman after one of his opening nights was taken aback by the author's rebuff when he ventured his opinion of the play.

"Perhaps you don't realize who I am?" said the man.

"That's only half of it," replied Kaufman.

During a fiery debate in the House of Representatives, one of the members from Illinois was pushing home his argument with great force and concluded with the words:

"I'm right. I know I'm right, so I say, with Henry Clay, sir, I would rather be right than be President."

Hearing this, Speaker Reed answered:

"The gentleman from Illinois will never be either."

Movie mogul Jed Harris had the disconcerting habit of occasionally greeting visitors stark naked. George S. Kaufman went to see him about the filming of one of his plays and brushed his full-frontal eccentricity aside by casually remarking: "Mr. Harris, your fly is open."

"I want to thank you, Mr. Marx, for all the enjoyment you've given the world," said a friendly old clergyman meeting Groucho for the first time.

"And I want to thank you for all the enjoyment you've taken out of it," replied Groucho.

The distinguished French writer Antoine de Rivarol was once asked his opinion of a couplet presented to him by an over-enthusiastic poet. After reading the two lines through several times, Rivarol handed them back to their author:

"Very nice, though there are dull stretches."

J UST A LINE

> I may be the first albino transvestite to become President, but I'm not a murderer—am I?

That's the first line of my first novel, and I hope you like it because it's as far as I've got.

With a novel that hopes to become a classic or a best seller (and I do want mine to be both), an arresting opening is essential. It may be just a line, but since it's got to grab the attention of the reader, it could claim to be the most important line in the book.

Here are the names of twenty successful novelists and the beguiling/intriguing/gripping opening sentences of twenty different novels. Can you decide who wrote what and give the title of each of the novels in question?

TWENTY NOVELISTS

Frederick Forsyth
F. Scott Fitzgerald
Gustave Flaubert
Agatha Christie
Jean Paul Sartre
Daphne du Maurier
John Steinbeck
George Orwell
Robert M. Pirsig
Laurence Sterne

Graham Greene
Franz Kafka
Leo Tolstoy
Norman Mailer
Charles Dickens
Jack Kerouac
L. P. Hartley
Ernest Hemingway
Virginia Woolf
Kurt Vonnegut

TWENTY NOVEL OPENINGS

1 Mr. Tench went out to look for his ether cylinder into the blazing Mexican sun and the bleaching dust.

2 The best thing would be to write down everything that happens from day to day.

3 Life goes on, yes—and a fool and his self-respect are soon parted, perhaps never to be reunited even on Judgment Day.

4 When the east wind blows up the Helford river the shining waters are troubled and disturbed, and the little waves beat angrily upon the sandy shores.

5 Robert Cohn was once middleweight boxing champion of Princeton.

6 London. Michaelmas Term lately over, and the Lord Chancellor sitting in Lincoln's Inn Hall. Implacable November weather.

7 Someone must have been spreading lies about Joseph K., for without having done anything wrong he was arrested one morning.

8 To the red country and part of the gray country of Oklahoma the last rains came gently, and they did not cut the scarred earth.

9 It was a bright cold day in April and the clocks were striking thirteen.

10 Nobody could sleep. When morning came, assault craft would be lowered and a first wave of troops would ride through the surf and charge ashore on the beach at Anopopei.

11 The past is a foreign country: they do things differently there.

12 I can see by my watch without taking my hand from the left grip of the cycle, that it is eight-thirty in the morning.

13 It was five o'clock on a winter's morning in Syria. Alongside the platform at Aleppo stood the train grandly designated in railway guides as the Taurus Express.

14 I first met Dean not long after my wife and I split up.

15 It is cold at six-forty in the morning of a March day in Paris, and seems even colder when a man is about to be executed by firing squad.

16 As the streets that lead from the Strand to the Embankment are very narrow, it is better not to walk down them arm-in-arm.

17 In the spring of 1917, when Doctor Richard Diner first arrived in Zurich, he was twenty-six years old, a fine age for a man, indeed the very acme of bachelorhood.

18 I wish either my father or my mother, or indeed both of them, as they were in duty equally bound to it, had minded what they were about when they begot me.

19 We were in the preparation room when the head came in, followed by a new boy in ordinary clothes, and by a school servant carrying a large desk.

20 All happy families resemble one another, but each unhappy family is unhappy in its own way.

(See Answers.)

I
BEFORE E?

When I taught English at the Park School in Baltimore, Maryland, I encouraged my students to learn what I had always regarded as one of the basic rules of spelling: "It's *I* before *E* except after *C*."

And so it is with *piece* and *receipt* and a multitude of other words. But unfortunately for me—and all the other English teachers who want a quiet life—it seems this time-honored rule isn't as reliable as we thought. The English language turns out to be riddled with words in which an *E* comes before an *I* and there's no *C* to be seen and in which an *I* comes before an *E* immediately after a *C*.

If you need proof that rules are made to be broken, here it is:

ageism	heifer	reimburse
agencies	heinous	rein
ancient	heir	reindeer
beige	Hygeia	reitbok
being	inveigle	science
Beirut	Keith	seize
caffeine	Leicester	sheik
codeine	leishmaniasis	Sheila
conscience	leisure	skein
counterfeit	Marcie	sleigh
deficient	mercies	sovereign
deign	monteith	species
Deirdre	neigh	sufficient
efficient	neighbor	surfeit
eider	Neil	tenancies
eighth	neither	their
either	nonpareil	theism
Fahrenheit	nuclei	unpolicied
fancied	obeisance	veiled
feign	omniscient	vein
feint	onomatopoeic	weigh
financier	pharmacopoeia	weir
foreign	plebeian	weird
forfeit	Pleiades	Weissnichtwo
freight	policies	zein
geisha	poltergeist	
glacier	proficient	

To make matters twice as bad, here are a dozen words where the golden rule is broken not once but twice:

alliciencies	efficiencies
anciencies	Einstein
cleidomancies	omnisciencies
deficiencies	oneiromancies

pleistoseist	sufficiencies
proficiencies	zeitgeist

Okay, so *Einstein*'s a name and *zeitgeist* isn't English, but you get the point—or is it *piont?* Spelling never was my strong suit.

A FINE SPELL

To find out how good you are at the spelling game, take a look at this list of fifty words. Alternative spellings are given for each word. What you have to do is work out which of the two versions is the correct one. A score of 20 is adequate for a high-school graduate, 30 is acceptable for a college graduate, 40 is excellent, and 50 unbelievable—or is it *unbeleivable?*

accomodation	accommodation	myrrh	myrhh
battallion	battalion	naphtha	naptha
broccoli	brocolli	occurrence	occurence
calender	calendar	parafin	paraffin
cemetary	cemetery	parallel	paralell
Chihuahua	Chihuhua	plausible	plausable
coliseum	colisseum	pseudonymous	pseudonymious
connoisseur	connoiseur	quintessence	quintessance
coxwain	coxswain	rarefy	rarify
desiccate	dessicate	reconnaissance	reconaissance
ecstasy	ecstacy	renaissance	rennaissance
elemosynary	eleemosynary	sacreligious	sacrilegious
embarass	embarrass	sangfroid	sangfroiod
fettucine	fettuccine	shillelagh	shilailie
gneis	gneiss	subpoenaed	subpoened
guilotine	guillotine	supersede	superseed
hemorhage	hemorrhage	threshhold	threshold
hypocricy	hypocrisy	ukelele	ukelelle
idiosyncrasy	idiosyncracy	vermillion	vermilion
jubilee	jubillee	vichysoise	vichyssoise
kwashiorkor	kwashiokor	victual	vitual

liaison	liasion	weltschmerz	welschmertz
liquefy	liquify	Xanthippe	Xanthipe
mischievous	mischeivous	yashmack	yashmak
moccasin	mocassin	zabagllione	zabaglione

(See Answers.)

ORIGINAL SPELLING

Some words look as if they have been misspelled when they haven't been. Here is a selection—or is it *sellection?*

Astroid is not a misspelling of *asteroid* but an adjective meaning "star-shaped."

Contect is not a misspelling of *context* but a verb meaning "to cover."

Crysal is not a misspelling of *crystal* but a part of an archery bow.

Galop is not a misspelling of *gallop* but a nineteenth-century German dance.

Harras is not a misspelling of *harrass* but a herd of stud horses.

Housebote is not a misspelling of *houseboat* but wood allowed to a tenant for repairing a house.

Merengue is not a misspelling of *meringue* but a popular Dominican and Haitian ballroom dance.

Orchestia is not a misspelling of *orchestra* but a genus of crustaceans, including beach fleas.

Orignal is not a misspelling of *original* but is the American moose.

Rictal is not a misspelling of *rectal* but an adjective meaning "relating to the mouth orifice."

Roadeo is not a misspelling of *rodeo* but a contest featuring events that test driving skill.

San Antonito is not a misspelling of *San Antonio* but a town in Bernalillo County, New Mexico.

Starlite is not a misspelling of *starlight* but a blue zircon, a type of mineral.

Tecnology is not a misspelling of *technology* but the study of children.

Tradevman is not a misspelling of *tradesman* but a petty officer in the U.S. Navy.

Viraginity is not a misspelling of *virginity* but the character of a virago—a bold, shrewish woman.

Warehous is not a misspelling of *warehouse* but the plural of *warehou*, a fish from Australia and New Zealand.

Warfarin is not a misspelling of *warfaring* but a chemical compound used as a rodenticide.

Windrow is not a misspelling of *window* but a row of hay, raked together to dry.

Zilwaukee is not a misspelling of *Milwaukee* but a town in Saginaw County, Michigan.

HYPHENATION HYPE

Words—like *half-life*—that use one hyphen are common enough. Words that need two hyphens—like *mother-in-law*—aren't unusual either. But finding words that require three hyphens or more isn't easy.

Here are mine, most of them names of plants or flowers:

3 HYPHENS

Snow-on-the-mountain is a spurge of the western United States that has showy flower clusters and is used ornamentally.

4 HYPENS

Gill-go-by-the-ground is a trailing Eurasian mint that is common as a weed in North America.

108

5 HYPHENS

John-go-to-bed-at-noon is any of several plants whose flowers close about noon.

Kiss-me-over-the-garden-gate is any of various plants, especially prince's-feather.

7 HYPHENS

Har-u-pu-ka-ka-sharu-sha-bau is the name of a mystical Egyptian deity.

8 HYPHENS

Willy-with-the-wisp-and-Peggy-with-the-lantern is a light that appears at night over marshy ground.

9 HYPHENS

Great-great-great-great-great-great-grand-niece-in-law is a relation; this particular term appears in the *Oxford English Dictionary* as an illustrative quotation given under *great* from John Lockhart's book *Reginald Dalton:* "that old body that says she is Shakespeare's great-great-great-great-great-great-grand-niece-in-law."

Kitty-come-down-the-lane-jump-up-and-kiss-me is the cuckoo-pint, a common European arum.

Meet-her-in-the-entry-kiss-her-in-the-buttery is another flower: a pansy.

The three words that have nine hyphens are the only three of their kind I've been able to find, and I have not come across a single word that has ten hyphens. If you happen to discover a not-four-five-six-seven-eight-or-nine-but-ten-legged word listed in any legitimate dictionary, do let me know.

G OOD AS GOLDFISH

Samuel Goldfish (1882–1974) had a winning way with words. Polish by birth, he became an American citizen, changed his name to Samuel Goldwyn, and grew to be one of the legendary Hollywood movie moguls. Almost as memorable as the great MGM pictures he produced were the great verbal clangers he created.

An agent once tried to sell Goldwyn a prominent actor. Goldwyn replied that he was not interested in established stars: He wanted to build his own stars instead.

"Look how I developed Jon Hall," said Goldwyn. "He's a better leading man than Robert Taylor will ever be—some day."

Goldwynisms are unique because they are turns of phrase that manage to make some sense and no sense at all at one and the same time. In my Goldwyn Book of Quotes these are the gems that would have pride of place.

"Every director bites the hand that lays the golden egg."

"A verbal contract isn't worth the paper it's written on."

"You ought to take the bull between the teeth."

"We're overpaying him but he's worth it."

"Why should people go out and pay good money to see bad films when they can stay at home and see bad television for nothing?"

"We have all passed a lot of water since then."

"How'm I gonna do decent pictures when all my good writers are in jail? Don't misunderstand me, they all ought to be hung."

"Chaplin is no businessman—all he knows is he can't take anything less."

"We want a story that starts with an earthquake and works its way up to a climax."

"My Toujours Lautrec!"

"Tell me, how did you love my picture?"

"Yes, my wife's hands are very beautiful. I'm going to have a bust made of them."

"Anybody who goes to see a psychiatrist ought to have his head examined."

When working on a motion picture of the life of Christ: "Why only twelve disciples? Go and get thousands."

"Gentlemen, I want you to know that I am not always right, but I am never wrong."

"If Roosevelt were alive he'd turn over in his grave."

"I'll give you a definite maybe."

"The reason why so many people turned up at Louis B. Mayer's funeral was they wanted to make sure he was dead."

"It's more than magnificent—it's mediocre."

"If you cannot give me your word of honor will you give me your promise?"

When told that a story was rather caustic he replied: "I don't care what it costs. If it's good, we'll make it."

Of a book: "I read part of it all the way through."

Of a piece of dialogue: "Let's have some new clichés."

"A bachelor's life is no life for a single man."

"A wide screen just makes a bad film twice as bad."

"Going to call him 'William'? What kind of a name is that? Every Tom, Dick and Harry's called William. Why don't you call him Bill?"

"In two words: im-possible."

F̲RENCH WITHOUT TEARS

Imagine the Lord talking French! Aside from a few odd words in Hebrew, I took it completely for granted that God had never spoken anything but the most dignified English.

Clarence Day was right. God speaks English—always has done, always will. And it's probably because they want to keep on the right side of the Almighty that the French have started to bring English words into their vocabulary.

The language of *haute cuisine* was once exclusively French, but nowadays at almost any Paris restaurant you can order *le fast food, le banana split, le biftek,* and *le chips*— which is what the English call french fries.

In the world of sport Frenchmen now speak of *le fair-play, le soccer,* and *les jockeys.* Sometimes their thinking gets a little muddled—*un jerk* is a good dancer, *un scratcher* is a great golfer, and *un egghead* is an imbecile—but on the whole they are on *le right track*.

Even their poetry is beginning to sound English. Read these three gems out loud and you will see—and hear—what I mean.

Un petit d'un petit
S'étonne aux Halles
Un petit d'un petit
Ah! degrés te fallent
Indolent qui ne sort cesse
Indolent qui ne se mène
Qu'importe un petit d'un petit
Tout Gai de Reguennes.

Reine, reine, guex éveille.
Gomme à gaine, en horreur, taie.

Oh, Anne, doux
But, Cueilles ma chou.
Trille fort,
Chatte dort.
Faveux Sikhs,
Pie coupe Styx.
Sève nette,
Les dèmes se traitent.
N'a ne d'haine,
Écoute, fée daine.

Éléphant tue elfes
Dit qu'en Delft.
Tartines, fortunes,
Miséricorde d'une.
Fit vetimes Sixtine
Médecine quitte Chine.
C'est Fantine est d'Inn
Mais Arouet dine.
Nanini, Toine est dit,
Met platres, sème petit.

E PISTLES AT DAWN

I once met a gambling man who had won a million dollars. I asked him what he did about all the begging letters. "Oh, I keep on sending them," he told me.

I'm not fond of begging letters, but I don't mind hate mail—so long as it's not addressed to me. I am a collector of caustic correspondence, and if you enjoy reading other people's acid epistles you'll like these.

TO THE EDITOR OF THE *KENYA STANDARD*:

Sir, if you print any more photographs of naked women, I shall cease borrowing your newspaper.

TO THE CBS TV NETWORK, NEW YORK:

What in hell is the matter with your news team?
What was so damned amusing about the item concerning

the lost mother cat with the amputated tail? To the concerned owners there was nothing very hilarious about it.

The whole news team repeatedly smirks and grins even after a report of a tragic incident in the news.

Don't tell me they have an irrepressible sense of humor. So do little boys and girls in the third grade.

TO COLUMNIST JOHN CARROLL, FROM AN ELVIS FAN, AFTER CARROLL HAD SUGGESTED ELVIS WAS PAST HIS PRIME:

To me your just a jealous old man who probably is ugly who would appreciate women screaming Jon Jon Jon we love you Jon. Well baby let me tell you you will get no where bad wrapping people.

And further more you have the power of the press backing you up a hundred percent so keep talking bad about people and you'll find nobody screaming Jon Jon we love you and remember there are other young reporters who might not like you who will talk bad about you and remember your tombstone might read
Jon Carroll the bad wrapper

TO CONSOLIDATED EDISON FOLLOWING THE BLACKOUT OF JULY 1977:

I just want to take the time to thank you for your two latest customer service ideas. I think the idea of using the intimacy of coziness and candlelight to bring New Yorkers together in our city's troubled times is a great one. And I also love your "instant home defrost service," wherein everyone in the city can defrost their freezers at the same time. I might also add that in this era of critical energy shortages, your new services are a great way to conserve vital energy supplies.

TO THE MASSACHUSETTS BOARD OF TAX ASSESSORS CONCERNING THE TAX LEVIED ON A VENERABLE VOLKSWAGEN:

Is this a joke? Or are you trying, with your traditional flair for subtlety, to tell us that our car is a closet Rolls-Royce, and is therefore going *up* in value? Whichever, this is not the season to be cute.

On the other hand, if you're seriously saying that our car is worth $4,550—your evaluation—please send us a check for that amount, or for anything even approaching that amount, and you can take delivery immediately. It would not be in our character to withhold from the state such an obvious treasure.

Indeed, such is our civic-minded zeal, we are prepared to make *you* an offer: if you can find anyone in the world who is willing to pay $4,550 for our car, we will gratefully sell it and pay precisely *double* the excise tax due. That is a solemn commitment. Think about it. How many taxpayers nowadays are prepared to *increase* their tax burden—voluntarily, at that—just to validate the simple but heartwarming notion that public employees know how to count?

So please let us have at once:

(1) Your check, whereupon we will give you possession of the car; or

(2) the check of the lucky person who is willing and able to pay $4,550 for the car, whereupon we will generously pay you double the excise due; or

(3) your reasons for not being able to come up with (1) or (2).

Believe me, the people of Massachusetts will never forget that at a time when public servants were widely considered to be venal nincompoops, you were courageous enough, shrewd enough, quick enough, to pick up an old VW for only $4,550 back before its market value really started skyrocketing.

TO GEORGE WASHINGTON FROM TOM PAINE:

As to you, sir, treacherous in private friendship, and a hypocrite in public life, the world will be puzzled to decide whether you are an impostate or an imposter; whether you have abandoned good principles, or whether you ever had any.

TO ABRAHAM LINCOLN AT THE WHITE HOUSE:

God damn your god damned old hellfired god damned soul to hell god damn you and god damn your god damned family's god damned hellfired god damned soul to hell and god damnation god damn them and god damn your god damned friends to hell.

TO PAUL HUME FROM HARRY S. TRUMAN FOLLOWING HUME'S UNFLATTERING REVIEW OF MARGARET TRUMAN'S SINGING:

I have just read your lousy review buried in the back pages. You sound like a frustrated old man who never made a success, an eight-ulcer man on a four-ulcer job, and all four ulcers working. I have never met you, but if I do you'll need a new nose and plenty of beefsteak and perhaps a supporter below. Westbrook

Pegler, a guttersnipe, is a gentleman compared to you. You can take that as more of an insult than as a reflection on your ancestry.

Top marx

Groucho Marx was one of the century's most prolific and entertaining letter writers. As a correspondent he was more quirky than caustic, as these four, very typical, letters show.

TO SAM ZOLOTOW OF *THE NEW YORK TIMES* DRAMA DEPARTMENT

December 5, 1945

Dear Sam,
My plans are still in embryo. In case you've never been there, this is a small town on the outskirts of wishful thinking. At the moment, I'm deep in the heart of *Casablanca* and it's thrilling work. I arise at seven every morning, kick the alarm clock in the groin and speed to the studio. I always get a nine o'clock call, which means I shoot promptly at three in the afternoon. There's no use protesting—this is the way the movie business is geared and I suspect that's the chief reason why so much bilge appears in your neighborhood theater.

Yours,
Groucho

TO HOWARD HUGHES

January 23, 1951

Dear Mr. Hughes,
Between retooling for the war effort and dueling with Wald and Krasna, I presume you are a fairly busy man. However, I wonder if you could spare a few moments to release a picture that was made some years ago involving Jane Russell, Frank Sinatra and your correspondent. The name of the picture, if memory serves, is *It's Only Money*. I never did see it but I have been told that at its various previews it was received with considerable enthusiasm.
I am not a young man anymore, Mr. Hughes, and before I

shuffle off this mortal coil if you could see your way clear to pry open the strong box and send this minor masterpiece whizzing through the film exchanges of America, you would not only have earned my undying gratitude but that of the United Nations, the popcorn dealers of America and the three RKO stockholders who at the moment are trying to escape from the Mellon Bank of Pittsburgh.

Sincerely,
Groucho Marx

TO T. S. ELIOT

June 19, 1961

Dear T. S.,

Your photograph arrived in good shape and I hope this note of thanks finds you in the same condition.

I had no idea you were so handsome. Why you haven't been offered the lead in some sexy movies I can only attribute to the stupidity of the casting directors.

Should I come to London I will certainly take advantage of your kind invitation and if you come to California I hope you will allow me to do the same.

Cordially,
Groucho Marx

TO M. LINCOLN SCHUSTER OF SIMON AND SCHUSTER, PUBLISHERS

September 13, 1963

Dear Lincoln,

How you ever came by that name is certainly beyond me. Not that it isn't a good name, but you must admit it is far removed from your last name.

Would you by any chance have the original manuscript of *Many Happy Returns,* a brilliant tome on the evils of taxation? It might have been the book of the year, except that shortly after it was published those little men in Tokyo blew Pearl Harbor to smithereens. (Frankly, I'm not sure what smithereens are, but it's a nice, long word and it gives even the most pedestrian letter [which this certainly is] a touch of class.)

Thanking you in advance, even if you can't find the manuscript. Yours until hell freezes over.

Groucho

LETTERS PLAY

Some of the most intriguing and important letters ever written weren't—if you see what I mean. Take a look at these historic documents, recently discovered by the historian and wit Michael Green.

From: Napoleon Bonaparte, Emperor of the French; First Consul for Life; First Citizen of France; King *in absentia* of the United Kingdom of Great Britain and Ireland; Commander-in-Chief of the Imperial Grand Army of France; Commander of the First Military District; Commander of the Second Military District; Commander of the Third Military District; Colonel-in-Chief of the Old Guard; Head of the Deuxième Bureau; Controller of the Troisième Bureau; Commander of the Légion d'Honneur; Chief of the Imperial Order of St. Anthony; holder of the Médaille Militaire with oak leaves; holder of the award for meritorious service (with branches).

To: The Empress Josephine of all France; Queen *in absentia* of the United Kingdom of Great Britain and Ireland; Grand Dame of the Imperial Order of St. Anthony.

Tilsit, Saturday

Tonight, Josephine.

Boney

From: The Empress Josephine of all France, Queen *in absentia* of the United Kingdom and Ireland; Grand Dame of the Imperial Order of St. Anthony.

To: Napoleon Bonaparte, Emperor of the French; First Consul for Life; First Citizen of France; King *in absentia* of the United Kingdom of Great Britain and Ireland; Commander-in-Chief of the Imperial Grand Army of France; Commander of the First Military District; Commander of the Second Military District; Commander of the Third Military District; Colonel-in-Chief of the Old Guard; Head of the Deuxième Bureau; Controller of the Troisième Bureau; Commander of the Légion d'Honneur; Chief of the Imperial Order of St. Anthony; holder of the Médaille Militaire with oak leaves; holder of the award for meritorious service (with branches).

Sorry, headache.

Josephine

To: General J. Custer
Commanding 7th Cavalry U.S. Army

Thursday

Sir,

I have the honor to report that in accordance with your instructions I have thoroughly scouted the area around little Big Horn and beg to report there are no signs of any Indians.

J. Adams (Lieut.)

Cherry Farm
Washington
Virginia
August 5, 1752

Dear Benjamin Franklin,

I am returning the remains of your kite, which was found in my oak tree after your unfortunate accident last Saturday. If I may say so, I do not think it is a very safe thing to do to fly a kite in a thunderstorm. However, I hope you have recovered from the effects of the explosion by now and that your hair will grow again. I also enclose some ointment Mrs. Franklin may find soothing for her burns. If you need any timber for rebuilding, you have only to ask.

Yours sincerely,
Abe Wetherhead

P.S. There is no need to pay for the hogs. We were going to kill them anyway, although not in such a spectacular fashion.

University of Yale
July 4, 1920

Professor Rutherford
Cavendish Laboratory
Cambridge University
Cambridge

Dear Professor Rutherford,

About that formula of mine, $E = MC^2$. I'm sorry to tell you that I made a mistake. It is wrong. It should be $E = R^3 + \frac{2}{5}(X^2 - Y) + 1$.

If you use the old formula it blows up. I know. I tried it.

Sorry about this. Hope you haven't used too much time on the research.

Sincerely,
Albert Einstein

D̲UNROAMIN

Whatever you call it—Dunroamin or Buckingham Palace, San Clemente or Mon Repos—if you give your house a name you give it an extra dimension. Whether you live in a tiny apartment with just one room or the world's largest house (Biltmore House in Asheville, North Carolina) with 250 rooms, when you give your home a name you help give it an identity.

To help you name or rename your home, here are twenty suggestions. They are all names that belong to real houses/apartments, and I have supplied explanatory notes as appropriate.

Alcrest	After labor comes *rest*.
Bachelor's Adventure	A holiday home.
Billion	Owned by Bill and Marion.
Bonanza	Spanish for *prosperity*.

Copper Coin	What was left in the bank after the purchase.
Dalsida	Home of a *Dalmatian*, a *Siamese*, and a Great *Dane*.
Elveston	Anagram of *lovenest*.
Erzanmine	Ours.
Fortitoo	42.
Hangover Hall	Seen in Temperance Road.
Lucky Dip	Holiday house at the beach.
Mews Cottage	Home of pampered cat.
Morning Feeling	Occupied by the Munday family.
Spooks	Opposite the cemetery.
The Chimes	Home of the Bell family.
The Pride	Where the Lyons family lives.
The Struggle	A house you can't afford.
Tivuli	A back-spelling.
Traynes	Near the rail station.
The White House	A good address.

CRAZY CROSSWORDS

It's CROSS CRAZY WORDS. No it isn't. It's WORDY CROSS-CRAZES. No it isn't. It's COZY WORDSCARES. No it isn't. It's WORSE CRAZYCODES. No it isn't. It's *CRAZY CROSS-WORDS*. Yes it is!

THE WORLD'S SMALLEST CROSSWORD

The world's largest crossword was devised by a Belgian called Henri Blaise. It contained 25,000 squares, featured 7,748 clues, and took Monsieur Blaise eight years to compile. I wanted to share it with you, but I didn't have the room. The crossword grid alone measures nearly nineteen square feet.

Instead I am offering you an original puzzle of my own. It's the world's smallest crossword and comes complete with a couple of suitably cryptic clues.

ACROSS
1 Time of deranged pride encompassing nothing.

DOWN
1 A marriage portion from a small Dutch coin that I leave.

(See Answers.)

AN AUSTRALIAN CROSSWORD

Here's another unusual crossword, with cryptic clues to match.

ACROSS
1 Time spent Down Under.

DOWN
1 Soundly a measure of print.
2 Hear that one is in debt.
3 Hero found after being deserted by her.
4 Australian end.

(See Answers.)

AN IRISH CROSSWORD

4 Knock one anyway you like, and one will get it off one correctly.

(See Answers.)

A SIBILANT CROSSWORD

William Sunners loves the nineteenth letter of the alphabet, and here's a crossword of his to prove it.

ACROSS
1 Shrieks.
5 Stories.
10 Section.
14 Seclude.
15 Site.
16 Stint.
17 Select.
18 Sinister side.
19 Subdues.
20 Solution.
22 Schooled sufficiently.
24 Swallows sustenance.
26 Specific sum sought.
27 Solanaceous shrub.
31 Stormy sea swell.
35 Strong spite.
36 Screened sharpshooting.
38 Strained situation.
39 Shears.
41 Steeple.
43 Starch.
44 Salt.
46 Scarcely sufficient.
48 Situated.
49 Savage sovereign.
51 Startlers.
53 Strong shipbuilding staves.
55 Singer.
56 Settle; set; steady.
60 Speech.
64 Sewing stitch.
65 Sorrow.
67 Street, surface.
68 Seed shell.
69 Spear.
70 Sign.
71 Sound.
72 Stopper.
73 Sunken spot.

DOWN
1 Stupor.
2 Sanction.
3 Scholars.
4 Seethed.
5 Stoic sufferers.
6 Summit.
7 Sinners' structure.
8 Sharp; stinging.
9 Saw set.
10 Scares.
11 State.
12 Stinted sustenance.
13 Suggested substitute.
21 Sound sensitizers.
23 Sable.
25 Springs.
27 Studied simulation.
28 Stopped sitting.
29 Salamanders.
30 Stately scanned songs.
32 Sub-let.
33 Shakespearean sorrowful
   sovereign's son.
34 Soil strivers.
37 Semi-sacred song safeguarded.
40 Sevenfold.
42 Smooth surfaces prayer.
45 Spawns.
47 Snare.
50 Speak slanderously.
52 Stand.
54 Sacred.
56 Sorrowful statement.
57 Springbok-like species.
58 Stamp.
59 Sense.
61 Steel sheet.
62 Stove.
63 Servant's superior (slang).
66 Skillful skywayman.

(See Answers.)

AN ANAGRAMMATIC CROSSWORD

I asked my friend Dave Crossland to create a couple of tough puzzles for this chapter, and he hasn't let me down. In this one all the clues are cryptic, and the across solutions have to be made into anagrams before they are inserted in the diagram. For example, if the intermediate solution to an across clue was TACIT, the letters could be rearranged to form the actual answer, ATTIC. You will be relieved to know that the down solutions are normal.

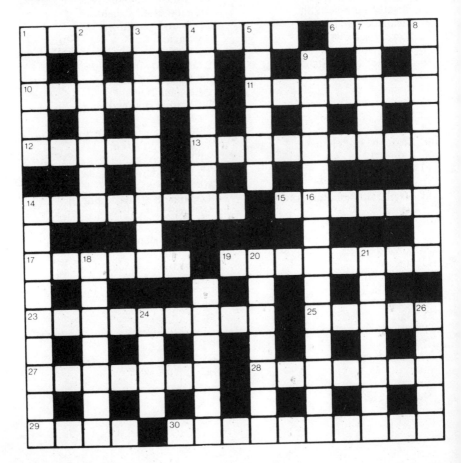

ACROSS

1 Very orderly worker is tense during heavy work? (10)
6 Fail to stand upright, being very thin. (4)
10 Rather rude convict, outwardly nonreligious. (7)
11 Save receipt, lady? That's mean. (7)
12 Sweeper having skirmish. (5)
13 Words put together to form courtly judgments. (9)
14 Full-time team in split. (8)
15 Bill joins two returning soaks. (6)
17 Lurking in steep lane there's a ceaseless traveler. (6)
19 Urgently wanting new design to include Rhode Island. (8)
23 Roman office gives praise about North America. (9)
25 Chemical temperature must be kept in check? Quite the reverse. (5)
27 Cyrus gets around the French displaying degree of attractiveness. (7)
28 Behold one, not completely elegant, dawdles. (7)
29 Observe a piece of music. (4)
30 To sing about milliner is causing great upset. (10)

DOWN

1 Exhibition of skills given by experts on piano. (5)
2 Neglects abandoned regions. (7)
3 Disease caused by parasites that orbit neck cunningly? (4–5)
4 Female turning up greets electorate, though not the whole lot. (7)
5 Appointing North American dynasty of old. (6)
7 Bowmen decapitated demonstrators. (7)
8 Conductor, one specially chosen, took a ride. (9)
9 Man of rank—king—raised dagger. (4)
14 I'm one in need of treatment, showing intolerance. (9)
16 Recovering, say, during exercise (having lost head). (9)
18 Foreigner, French one, thrown into a jail. (7)
20 Inactivity? Wrong, I train with small amount of energy. (7)
21 Plead, in old-fashioned way, during free entertainment. (7)
22 Most recent fashion stimulates trend within. (6)
24 I governed a country. (4)
26 Enchanted siren in more elevated place? (5)

(See Answers.)

A CROSSWORD WITH MISPRINTS

There is a misprint of one letter in the definition part of each across clue (e.g., if the definition word was printed as DENTAL, the correct definition might be DENIAL). Answers are to be inserted correctly. Down clues are normal, but solutions are to be entered with one letter misprinted: The misprinted letter occurs always where the down word intersects with an across one, and the misprinted form of the solution is always a word in its own right.

ACROSS

1 Chap, Canadian, is thinner. (7)
5 Established in fort, actors took charge. (7)
9 Result of mending cord—first pull one on. (9)
10 Hastily elect leaders of the Unionist Party after race. (3, 2)
11 Receives black sections of sail. (6)
12 I caper and pass wanderer hiding identity. (8)
14 Smells in apartments around the East. (8)
15 Shell guided first pair of geologists. (5)
18 Chimp gives fwee entertainment, it's said. (5)
20 Snows at hand on the Sabbath. (8)
23 First person, we hear, dances in stages. (8)
25 Very cold coves, one centigrade—take a step back. (3–3)
27 Food means nothing in early part of day. (5)
28 Trap siren with cunning, and swear. (9)
29 Gentleman trapped in action is wasted. (7)
30 Striker observed lots of people on backstreet in Paris. (7)

DOWN

1 Regions of one hundred fruit trees. (6)
2 Wealth enables a barrier to be put around virus. (9)
3 Attentive male sorted out feud over lady. (7)
4 South African currency obtained in Iran, dubiously. (4)
5 Came to an agreement (abridged?). (10)
6 Freed from sin, shiver, trembling, before last part of absolution. (7)
7 Satan, rising up, was far from dead. (5)
8 Gave account that went off with a bang? (8)
13 Made report about one tailless hybrid being aroused. (10)
16 I have gone on to desert the cause, showing signs of imperfection. (9)
17 Rushed, upset. (8)
19 Short film of mobile home. (7)
21 Imprisons first of ghosts during awful seance. (7)
22 University supporting army regulation creates commotion. (6)
24 Cautions, normal in battles. (5)
26 Steady business enterprise. (4)

(See Answers.)

A FLUID CROSSWORD

1	2	3	4	5
6				
7				
8				
9				

ACROSS

1 A hunchbacked puppet with a hooked nose.
6 A short-legged round-bodied horse bred in England.
7 To drive cattle in the U.S.A.
8 To thump or strike.
9 A type of tool.

DOWN

1 Sound vegetables.
2 Sound sheep.
3 Sound measures of print.
4 Sound of Black, Red, White, and Yellow marine regions.
5 Hydrogen in brief, times five.

And why is it a *fluid* crossword?

(See Answers.)

BURGER POWER

Gazing at the typewriter in moments of desperation ("Mrs. Beeton died at twenty-eight. I'm thirty-four and what have I done?"), hitting the typewriter in moments of black despair ("Keats died at twenty-five; I'm pushing forty, and what have I done?"), I console myself with three thoughts: a drink at six, dinner at eight, and to be immortal you've got to be dead.

I'm alive and I adore food and drink. To me they're very real pleasures indeed (and I'm delighted to hear from my elders that they're also the pleasures that last), and because I find them such fun I'm able to use food as a carrot and drink as a carrot juice (?) in the never-ending struggle to get my work done. As writers go, I'm quite disciplined: I set myself a target of so many words an hour, and if I get behind schedule I don't give myself a break until I've caught up. On "writing days" I have a light lunch and never drink until the day's work is done. With my first book, I had a celebratory meal at the end of every chapter. Now I've written so many, I don't celebrate until the whole book is done.

In the matter of food, as with everything else, I'm a very lucky individual. I live with one of the world's great cooks. I eat like a king—quite literally, at times, since my wife has made a specialty of the favorite dishes of English monarchs since the Norman Conquest. Here's a recipe for a princely dessert that I love! I admit that "Quyncys in Compost" isn't the most appetizing of titles, but once tried it's never forgotten. And it's a dish that's stood the test of time: Henry VI (aged eight) had it at his Coronation banquet in 1422.

You will need: 2½ ounces whole stem ginger; 3 fluid ounces sherry wine; 22 fluid ounces red wine; 4 quinces or large, firm pears; 8 ounces caster sugar; 8 ounces stoned dates; 2 level teaspoons ground cinnamon; 1 level teaspoon ground ginger; a pinch of salt.

Cut the ginger into thin slices and leave to soak in the sherry in a covered jar for three days.

Peel the quinces or pears and slice into rounds about one-quarter inch thick. Remove core from each piece of fruit. Dissolve the sugar gently in the wine and heat until the syrup starts to thicken (about 15 minutes). Add the fruit to the wine and simmer gently until cooked but still firm (about 10 minutes). Add the dates, spices, and salt. Continue heating without boiling until the flavors are thoroughly blended. Taste, and add more sugar if necessary. The wine should have a syrupy consistency and the fruit should be firm. Leave to cool.

Strain the ginger, reserving a tablespoon of the liquid. Stir this and the ginger into the wine syrup. Serve well chilled. (*Serves 6.*)

When I'm not eating like an English king, I'm eating like a modern American. Man cannot live by bread alone, which is why he puts meat next to it and calls it a hamburger. There must be Macdonald blood in my veins, because show me a burger and my mouth starts to water. What's more, not only do I eat burgers of every kind with relish (and without), I also collect their names.

Here are forty that I've come across. Lick your lips and read on:

baconburger

barbecueburger

beefburger

catfish-burger*

cheeseburger

chicken-burger

chile-burger

Chinese-burger (containing rice)

chuckburger

clamburger

dogburger

double-burger (two hamburgers in one bun)

eggburger

fishburger

glutenburger*

griddleburger (browned on a griddle)

horsemeatburger*

huskiburger*

jamburgo (a Mexican spelling of *hamburger*—not a hamburger served with jam)

kirschburger*

lamburger (made of ground lamb)

liver-sausage-burger

liverwurst-burger

nutburger

oomphburger (a hamburger served with oomph!)

pickleburger

porkburger

rabbitburger*

seaburger*

Spamburger (made from a proprietary ground meat, Spam)

tomatoburger

*These I've heard about but haven't eaten. All the rest I unreservedly recommend.

AIEEEEEE

A IEE!

I like unusual words, and the more unusual they are the more I like them. That's why I've leafed through *Webster's Third New International Dictionary* to find the hundred most unusual and—to me—most likable words in the English language.

Here they are:

aiee	An interjection of grief.
axolotl	A salamander.
bdelloid	Like a leech.
cnemial	Relating to the shin.
crwth	An ancient Celtic musical instrument.
csardas	A Hungarian dance.
ctetology	A branch of biology.

cwm	A basin on a mountainside.
dghaisa	A small boat of Malta.
dhikr	A ritual formula.
dirndl	A style of dress.
djebel	A hill in northern Africa.
dukhn	A cereal grass of Africa and Asia.
dukw	An amphibious vehicle.
dvandva	A compound word.
dwam	To become dazed.
dzeren	A gazelle of Asia.
eebree	An eyebrow.
Firbolg	An early people of Ireland.
forjaskit	Exhausted.
fremd	Unrelated.
gjetost	A hard dark-brown cheese made from goat's milk.
gmelinite	A mineral.
gwyniad	A Welsh fish.
gyttja	A type of mud containing organic material.
hamsocn	Burglary or housebreaking.
hheth	The eighth letter of the Hebrew alphabet.
hjelmite	A mineral.
hsin	In Confucianism, the cardinal virtue of faithfulness.
humuhumunukunu-kuapuaa	A small Hawaiian fish.
hwan	The basic monetary unit of South Korea.
iao	An Australian bird.
ieie	A pine of the Pacific Islands.
ioa	A sea bird chiefly found in tropical seas.
ixodid	A tick.
iynx	A woodpecker.

jheel	A pool, marsh, or lake of India.
jnana	Knowledge.
kjeldahlization	A particular chemical process.
Kpelle	A people of central Liberia.
Kshatriya	A twice-born Hindu.
kthibh	A type of reading in the Hebrew Bible.
kvass	A beer.
Kwalhioqua	A people of southwestern Washington State.
kokerboom	The quiver tree.
kwatuma	Any of several eels of southern Africa.
kyoodle	To holler, to yap.
lamedh	The twelfth letter of the Hebrew alphabet.
Lwena	A Bantu language.
mbori	A camel disease.
mlechchha	One who does not practice Hinduism.
Mpongwe	Another Bantu language.
msasa	Any of various African trees.
mwami	The native ruler or king of Ruanda-Urundi, Africa.
Mzabite	A Berber people of the Algerian Sahara.
naumkeag	A machine for smoothing the soles and heels of shoes.
ngege	An important African food fish.
njave	A very large tropical African tree.
Nkole	Another Bantu language.
nritya	A type of dance of India, Asia.
nsambya	An African timber tree.
ollamh	A learned man in ancient Ireland.
o-o-a-a	A bird from the Hawaiian island of Kauai.
ouabaio	A tree of southern Africa.
piobaireachd	Elaborate tunes for the Scottish Highland bagpipes.

pneumonoultra-microscopicsilico-volcanoconiosis	A miner's lung disease.
qutb	An Islamic saint.
ramfeezled	Exhausted.
rsi	A holy Hindu sage.
rta	A specific principle.
sdrucciola	A musical term.
sferics	Atmospherics.
sjogrenite	A mineral.
smaragd	Emerald.
squdge	Ooze.
sravaka	A direct disciple of Buddha.
szikite	A mineral.
tehaviche	The king salmon.
tfillin	The phylacteries worn by Jews.
tjaele	Frozen ground.
tlac	A small copper coin of nineteenth-century Mexico.
tmesis	Separation of the parts of a compound word.
tnoyim	A Jewish social function.
tomnoddy	A fool.
tryptyque	A customs pass.
tsantsa	A shrunken head.
tzut	A brightly patterned square of cotton worn as a head covering.
uang	A rhinoceros beetle.
ucuuba	A Brazilian tree.
uwarowite	An emerald-green garnet.
vly	A temporary lake.
voeu	A proposal.
vrille	An airplane maneuver.
yclept	Named.
ynambu	A very large bird of southern Brazil.

yperite	Mustard gas.
yttrium	A chemical element.
zikr	The same as *dhikr*.
zloty	The basic monetary unit of Poland.
zwieback	A sweetened bread.

UNIQUE DARRYL

I like dictionaries, but my friend Darryl Francis is demented about them. Recently he waded through fifteen of the world's leading English dictionaries simply to find a word in each that wasn't in any of the others.

Locating one word that is unique to each of the fifteen dictionaries was no easy task. Selecting a likely word from a particular dictionary and then checking it against the other fourteen usually revealed that the word *did* appear in at least one of the others—often the twelfth, thirteenth, or fourteenth. In his search Darryl made countless false starts. For example, he thought *gallerygoer* was unique to *Webster's New Collegiate* (9th edition) until he found the hyphenated form, *gallery-goer*, in the *Oxford English Dictionary*, though not as a main entry. He thought *Eastralia* was unique to the 1909 edition of *Webster's* until he found it tucked away in the supplement to the *Century Dictionary*. *Kgotla*, in the H–N Supplement of the *Oxford English Dictionary*, looked like it might be unique, but it then turned up in *Chambers*. He expected *complexification* in the 1934 *Webster's* to be unique as it hadn't been included in the 1961 *Webster's*, but no! The A–G Supplement of the *Oxford English Dictionary* also lists *complexification*.

Darryl is one of those verbivores who doesn't give in easily and eventually he made it. Thanks to his persistence, *More Joy of Lex* can now proudly present the fifteen unique words that are featured once and once only in fifteen of the world's most important dictionaries.

Here they are:

The Century Dictionary (1897)

bamlite   A variety of fibrolite, a subsilicate of aluminium, from Bamle, Norway.

The Century Dictionary Supplement (1909)

pisang-ayer   The traveler's-tree of the East Indies.

Chambers Twentieth Century Dictionary (1977)

gju   A kind of violin used in the Shetland Isles of Scotland.

Concise Oxford Dictionary (6th edition, 1976)

antivivisectionism   Opposition to vivisection.

Funk & Wagnall's New Standard Dictionary (1946)

zij   The Persian astronomical tables, revised and corrected by Omar Khayyam.

The Oxford English Dictionary (1933)

steeplet   A small steeple.

Supplement to *The Oxford English Dictionary* (1933)

witchologist   One who studies witches or witchcraft.

A–G Supplement to *The Oxford English Dictionary* (1972)

deproletarianizable   Able to be freed of proletarian character or qualities.

H–N Supplement to *The Oxford English Dictionary* (1976)

jazzophile   A devotee of jazz.

Random House Dictionary (1966)

fiqh   In Islam, jurisprudence based on theology.

Webster's New International Dictionary (1st edition, 1909)

fabrikona   A variety of canvas wall hanging.

Webster's New International Dictionary (2nd edition, 1934)

Taeniodontidae   A family of Lower Eocene edentates, certain toothless prehistoric mammals.

Webster's Third New International Dictionary (1961)

rta   The cosmic-moral principle of order that in Vedic tradition establishes regularity and righteousness in the world.

Webster's New Collegiate Dictionary (8th edition, 1973)

buqsha   A monetary unit of the Yemen, 40 buqshas to the rial.

Collins English Dictionary (1979)

twp   A Welsh dialect word meaning "stupid."

MISH MASH

Darryl Francis has learned a lot by reading dictionaries. Dr. Frederick C. Mish has learned a lot writing them. He is joint editorial director of the Merriam-Webster family of dictionaries and has taught me almost all I know about etymology, including the fact that it's the study of the history and origin of words and comes from the Greek *etymon* meaning "true meaning."

Over a cup of coffee he kindly explained that *coffee* comes from the Italian *caffe*, which derives from the Turkish word *kahve*, which in turn comes from the Arabic *quahwah*. He also revealed that *catsup* comes from the Malay word *kechap*, meaning "spiced fish sauce." *Bamboo* is also from a Malay word spelled *bambu*. From Tahitian we get *tatoo*, which means the same in Tahiti as it does at home. The Chinese gave us *tea*, and from the Persian comes *shawl*.

"Quite often," according to Dr. Mish, "when the first settlers in a country found something new, they simply adopted the native word for it. When the first English settlers spotted what the Algonquian Indians called an *arahkun*, they took the Indian word and made it *raccoon*. In fact, the American Indian gave us such words as *persimmon*, *hickory*, *caucus*, and many others."

Here are some more Mish marvels selected at random from the international melting pot of words. The word *goulash* is a good old Hungarian word, *gulyas*, meaning "herdsman's stew." The Finns invented the *sauna*, and we have their word for it. *Cashew* came from the Portuguese. *Pastrami* is from the Rumanian *pastrama* by way of Yiddish. And *whiskey* is from the Irish Gaelic and Scottish Gaelic—of course!

Dorothy Lamour wore one and made it famous, and the word for *sarong* comes from the Malay *kain sarong*, meaning "a cloth sheath." *Shampoo* is from the Hindi; *molasses* from Portuguese; *hanker* probably from Flemish; and *boomerang* is a native name in Australia.

Swastika is not a German word, despite its having been made famous by Hitler. It is from Sanskrit. In fact, the sign itself is an old one and is found in many civilizations.

Our word *pal* is from the Romany *phal*, which means "brother or friend." Romany is the Indic language of the Gypsies. *Pariah* is from Tamil, in which language it literally means "drummer" and refers to a member of a low caste of southern India and Burma. We use the word to mean "outcast." *Kowtow* is from the Chinese and means, literally, "to bump the head."

The word *kosher* is from Yiddish and came in turn from Hebrew where it meant "fit, proper." The word *khaki* is from the Hindi and means "dust-colored" in that language. *Mammoth* comes from the Russian word *mamont; thug* is from the Hindi word for thief; *sleigh* from the Dutch; and *assassin* from the Arabic *hashshashin,* which means "one addicted to hashish."

The word *penguin* may come from the Welsh *pen gwyn,* meaning "white head." *Pajama* is from the Hindi, and *robot* from the Czech, meaning "work." The name for our old friend the chimpanzee comes from a word in the Kongo dialect. And *taboo* comes from the Tonga Islands of the Southwest Pacific. In Tongan, *tabu* is something "charged with a dangerous supernatural power and forbidden to profane use."

Origin unknown

Dr. Mish is a very clever man. He can give you the etymology of almost every word in the language, but some words have beaten him. And not just him. There are certain English words whose etymologies are unknown. Here are forty of the words that have defeated the dictionary-makers. If you can shed any light on the mystery of their origin, Dr. Mish would like to hear from you.

barf	To vomit.
boffin	Scientific expert.
bonkers	Crazy, mad.
clobber	To pound, to defeat.
codswallop	Nonsense.
dido	Prank.
dildo	Penis substitute.
dingleberry	A shrub.
faggot	Homosexual.
flub	To botch.
gizmo	A gadget.
gunnel	A fish.
hickey	A device.
hootenanny	A gathering at which folk singers entertain.
jive	Swing music.
kludge	A system made up of components that are poorly matched.
lobbygow	An errand boy.
lummox	A clumsy person.
lunker	Something large of its kind.
malarkey	Bunkum.
moola	Money.
pemoline	A synthetic organic drug.
pen	A female swan.
raddled	Being in a state of confusion.
rampike	Erect, broken or dead tree.
raunchy	Slovenly, dirty.
rolamite	A nearly frictionless elementary mechanism.
scag	Heroin.
scrim	A durable fabric.
shandrydan	Chaise with a hood.
shim	Thin piece of material.
slather	A great quantity.
snaffle	To obtain, especially by devious means.

snitch	To inform.
toke	A puff on a marijuana cigarette.
trangam	A trinket, or gimcrack.
twat	Vulva.
twerp	A silly person.
willies	A fit of nervousness.
zonked	Being under the influence of alcohol.

A
NGELICAL ASPIRATES

Take a letter. Add another letter to make a word. Add a third letter to make a new word. Keep on adding letters and making longer words until you have to stop.

Here's how it's done:

A	The first letter of the alphabet.
AN	The indefinite article.
ANG	The hairy part of an ear of barley.
ANGE	Trouble, affliction, anguish.
ANGEL	A celestial spirit.
ANGELI	A town in Sweden.
ANGELIC	Having the nature of an angel.

ANGELICA	A sweet dessert wine produced in California.
ANGELICAL	Having the nature of an angel.
ANGELICALS	Nuns of an extinct order established in Milan in 1530.

B	The second letter of the alphabet.
BU	An old Japanese gold coin.
BUT	A conjunction.
BUTT	A large cask.
BUTTE	An isolated hill or small mountain.
BUTTER	An important food.
BUTTERI	The surname of an Italian painter, 1540–1606.
BUTTERIN	A reformed spelling of *butterine*.
BUTTERINE	An imitation butter.
BUTTERINES	The plural of *butterine*.
BUTTERINESS	The quality of being buttery.

B	The second letter of the alphabet.
BI	Bisexual.
BIT	A piece.
BITT	A post on a ship's deck.
BITTE	A spelling of *bit* used in the fourteenth, fifteenth and sixteenth centuries.
BITTER	Sharp.
BITTERN	Any of various small and medium-sized herons.
BITTERNE	A seventeenth-century spelling of *bittern*.
BITTERNES	The plural of *bitterne*.
BITTERNESS	The quality of being bitter.
BITTERNESSE	An old spelling of *bitterness*.
BITTERNESSES	The plural of *bitterness*.

Now try doing it the other way around, putting the new letter in front of the first letter.

E	The fifth letter of the alphabet.
TE	A musical tone.
ATE	The past tense of *eat*.
RATE	A charge, payment, or price.
IRATE	Angry.
PIRATE	A robber on the high seas.
SPIRATE	Voiceless.
ASPIRATE	To pronounce with an *h* sound.

Build this one on your own.

__	The fifth letter of the alphabet.
__ __	A musical tone.
__ __ __	The past tense of *eat*.
__ __ __ __	A lock of hair.
__ __ __ __ __	Condition.
__ __ __ __ __ __	A social or political class.
__ __ __ __ __ __ __	To state in a new form.
__ __ __ __ __ __ __ __	In Roman and civil law, to perform.

(See Answers.)

Here is another attractive arrangement of words. In the pattern on the left, the words *end* with all the different letters of the alphabet, progressing from A to Z, with their lengths varying from 1 to 13 letters and from 13 back to 1. In the pattern on the right, the words *begin* with all the different letters of the alphabet, progressing from A to Z, with their lengths varying from 1 to 13 and from 13 back to 1.

A	A
OB	BE
SAC	CAT
LEAD	DIME
PLATE	ELECT
SCRUFF	FIERCE
MORNING	GROCERY
HAWFINCH	HORRIBLE
SPAGHETTI	INORGANIC
DARYAOGANJ	JUXTAPOSED
STICKLEBACK	KLEPTOMANIA
TETRARCHICAL	LIQUEFACTION
PARALLELOGRAM	MICROSCOPICAL
ACCREDITATION	NEFARIOUSNESS
WHILLABALLOO	OBSTREPEROUS
THUNDERCLAP	PALINDROMIC
QARAQALPAQ	QUADRUPLET
GODMOTHER	ROUGHNECK
SLOWNESS	SYMPHONY
CONTENT	THEREIN
BUREAU	UNDONE
SCLAV	VOICE
SLOW	WILD
BOX	XED
MY	YE
Z	Z

Daryoganj is the name of a town in India; *Qaraqalpaq* is a Turkic people of Central Asia; *Sclav* is a variant spelling of *Slav*, a person who speaks a Slavic language; and *xed* means "marked with a cross."

B
AA BAA BANANA!

There are numerous words that use a particular letter twice. For example, *there* has two *E*s, *numerous* has two *U*s, *particular* has two *A*s and two *R*s, and *letter* has two *E*s and two *T*s. Here is an A to Z of words in which the same letter appears twice.

a	*baa*	n	*inn*
b	*ebb*	o	*coo*
c	*cock*	p	*pup*
d	*did*	q	*quinquennium*
e	*bee*	r	*err*
f	*off*	s	*ass*
g	*gag*	t	*tot*
h	*high*	u	*usual*

i	iris	v	viva
j	jejune	w	wow
k	kick	x	executrix
l	all	y	yolky
m	mum	z	jazz

A *quinquennium* is a five-year period; *viva* is an interjection of good will; and *executrix* is a female executor.

Compiling an A to Z of words in which the same letter appears three times is more difficult, but it can be done.

a	banana	n	nanny
b	bobby	o	ovolo
c	coccyx	p	poppy
d	daddy	q	Qaraqalpaq
e	epee	r	error
f	fluff	s	sass
g	gaggle	t	tatty
h	heighth	u	unusual
i	iiwi	v	viva-voce
j	Jijjin	w	powwow
k	kakariki	x	hexahydroxycyclohexane
l	lull	y	syzygy
m	mummy	z	zizz

Heighth is a dialectal spelling of *height; iiwi* is a brightly colored Hawaiian bird; *Jijjin* is a town in Jordan; *kakariki* is both a parrakeet and a lizard from New Zealand; *Qaraqalpaq* is a Turkic people of Central Asia; and *hexahydroxycyclohexane* is a chemical, a member of the vitamin B complex, which is essential for life; and *zizz* is a whirring sound.

A complete A to Z of words in which the same letter is repeated four times is impossible. With V and X I failed, but I did my best with the rest.

a	maharaja	n	nonunion
b	bubbybush	o	voodoo

c	*scacchic*	p	*whippersnapper*
d	*diddled*	q	*Qawiqsaqq*
e	*teepee*	r	*recurrer*
f	*riffraff*	s	*assess*
g	*gagging*	t	*statuette*
h	*high-thoughted*	u	*muumuu*
i	*visibility*	v	*???*
j	*jejunojejunostomy*	w	*wow-wow*
k	*kakkak*	x	*???*
l	*pellmell*	y	*fyyryryn*
m	*mummydom*	z	*razzmatazz*

A *bubbybush* is another name for the strawberry shrub; *scacchic* means "relating to chess"; *high-thoughted* is merely having high thoughts; a *jejunojejunostomy* is the operative formation of a passage between two portions of the jejunum, part of the small intestine; a *kakkak* is a small bittern from the island of Guam; *Qawiqsaqq* is the name of a particular bluff in Alaska; a *muumuu* is a loose dress worn mainly in Hawaii; a *wow-wow* is any of several gibbons; *fyyryryn* is a Middle English spelling of fire iron.

You won't be surprised to learn that I couldn't find words containing five Js, Qs, Vs, or Xs, but I managed the rest of the alphabet.

a	*abracadabra*	n	*nonintervention*
b	*hubble-bubble*	o	*oronooko*
c	*circumcrescence*	p	*pepper-upper*
d	*fuddy-duddy*	q	*???*
e	*telemetered*	r	*terror-stirring*
f	*fluffy-ruffle*	s	*assesses*
g	*wiggle-waggling*	t	*totipotentiality*
h	*High-Churchmanship*	u	*Uburu-uku*
i	*illimitability*	v	*???*
j	*???*	w	*M'daywawkawntwawns*
k	*Kvikkjokk*	x	*???*

l	*lillypilly*	y	*gryffygryffygryffs*
m	*mmm'mm*	z	*Zzzzz*

A *hubble-bubble* is a flurry of activity; a *circumcrescence* is a growing over; *fluffy-ruffle* is an adjective meaning with fluffy ruffled margins; *Kvikkjokk* is a town in Sweden; *lillypilly* is an Australian tree with hard, fine-grained wood; *mmm'mm* is sex appeal; *oronooko* is a type of tobacco; *totipotentiality* is a biological term, the capability of developing along any of the lines inherently possible; *Uburu-uku* is a place in Nigeria; *M'day-wawkawntwawns* are Indians of the Dakota people, a name more frequently spelled *Mdewakantons; gryffygryffygryffs* comes from James Joyce's *Finnegans Wake*, about two-thirds of the way through chapter 11; and *Zzzzz* is the name of a wake-up service in Los Angeles.

SEEING DOUBLE

Words in which the same letter appears twice and together are common enough. *Common*, with its double *M*, is one of them. Can you compile a list of twenty-six words in each of which a different letter of the alphabet appears twice and together? *JJ, QQ, XX*, and *YY* are the tough ones.

(See Answers.)

THREE'S COMPANY

Finding words in which the same letters appear three, four, or more times in a row is a challenge, but I like to think I'm equal to it.

Kaaawa is the name of a town on the island of Oahu in Hawaii; and *Faaa* is the name of a settlement on the west coast of Tahiti.

The Oxford English Dictionary contains *weeest*, the superlative form of *wee*, in an illustrative quotation dating from 1878; the same dictionary also includes *seeer*, "one who sees."

The American Thesaurus of Slang contains the three words *pfff*, *pffft*, and *phffft*, all meaning "to go to ruin."

The exclamation *shhh*, requesting silence, seems common enough, but no dictionary actually deigns to list it. *Hmmm* does appear in dictionaries of slang and is an expression of pleasure or astonishment.

The straightforward *frillless*, without a frill, is given in *The Oxford English Dictionary*; and the similar *wallless* is in an earlier edition of the unabridged Webster's.

Brrr is expressive of shivering with cold or apprehension and appears in the 1972 Supplement to *The Oxford English Dictionary*.

There are several examples of three- *S* words. *The Oxford English Dictionary* contains *countessship*, *duchessship*, and *goddessship*, while its 1972 Supplement contains *bossship*. An earlier edition of *Webster's* gives both *headmistressship* and *patronessship*.

The *Oxford* offers two words with three *U*s: *vertuuus*, a fourteenth-century spelling of *virtuous*, and *uuula*, an early form of *uvula*.

Bzzzbzzz is given in *The American Thesaurus of Slang* as a synonym for *gossip*.

Four *A*s appear in *Aaaahtamad*, the name of an unidentified town in ancient Palestine.

Eeeeve is the local name of the Hawaiian bird *iiwi*.

Four *O*s appear in the curious *Cookkoooose*, a name given to the tribes of the Kusan Indian family.

Four *S*s appear in the palindromic *esssse*, an old spelling of *ashes*, which is given as a main entry in *The Oxford English Dictionary*. And *zzzz* is given as a verb, "to snore," in *The American Thesaurus of Slang*.

The American Thesaurus of Slang also has *00000* as an exclamation of surprise. In the eighteenth century, there was a British racehorse called *POTOOOOOOOO*. This was pronounced *potatoes*, made up from *pot* and *eight Os*.

The most extreme example to appear in print is in Philip Roth's best-selling *Portnoy's Complaint*. On the last page is a howl of anguish, represented by 231 consecutive *A*s, followed by four *H*s. Thus:

AAAAAAAAAAAAAAAAAAAAAAAAAAAAAAAAAAAAAA-
AAAAAAAAAAAAAAAAAAAAAAAAAAAAAAAAAAAAAA-
AAAAAAAAAAAAAAAAAAAAAAAAAAAAAAAAAAAAAA-
AAAAAAAAAAAAAAAAAAAAAAAAAAAAAAAAAAAAAA-
AAAAAAAAAAAAAAAAAAAAAAAAAAAAAAAAAAAAAA-
AAAAAAAAAAAAAAAAAAAAAAAAAAAAAAAAAAAAAA-
AAAAAAAAAAAAAAAAAAAAAHHHH

Beat that!

CRITICAL CRITICS

As playwright Christopher Hampton once said: "Asking a working actor what he thinks about critics is like asking a lamp-post how it feels about dogs." It does happen and some playwrights have a ready answer. This was Brendan Behan's: "Critics are like eunuchs in a harem. They're there every night, they see it done every night, they see how it should be done every night, but they can't do it themselves."

The heyday of corruscating criticism in America was also the heyday of the Algonquin Round Table. The Table's leading lady, Dorothy Parker, managed to sum up one play in five words: "*House Beautiful* is play lousy." She was often as caustic but not always so concise. Here she is reviewing Margot Asquith's *Lay Sermons:*

In this book of essays, which has all the depth and glitter of a worn dime, the Countess walks right up to such subjects as Health, Human Nature, Fame, Character, Marriage, Politics, and Opportunities. A rather large order, you might say, but it leaves the lady with unturned hair. Successively, she knocks down and drags out each topic. And there is something vastly stirring in the way in which, no matter where she takes off from, she brings the discourse back to Margot Asquith. Such single-ness of purpose is met but infrequently.

When she does get around to less personal matters, it turns out that her conclusions are soothingly far from startling. A compilation of her sentiments, suitably engraved upon a nice, big calendar, would make an ideal Christmas gift for your pastor, your dentist, or Junior's music teacher. Here, for instance, are a few ingots lifted from her golden treasury: "The artistic temperament has been known to land people in every kind of dilemma . . ." "Pleasure will always make a stronger appeal than Wisdom . . ." "It is only the fine natures that profit by Experience . . ." "It is better to be a pioneer than a passenger, and best of all to try and create . . ." "It is not only what you See but what you Feel that kindles appreciation and gives life to Beauty . . ." "Quite apart from the question of sex, some of the greatest rascals have been loved . . ." "I think it is a duty women owe not only to themselves, but to everyone else, to dress well."

The Thames, I hear, remains as damp as ever in the face of these observations.

Through the pages of *Lay Sermons* walk the great. I don't say that Margot Asquith actually permits us to rub elbows with them ourselves, but she willingly shows us her own elbow, which has been, so to say, honed on the mighty. "I remember President Wilson saying to me"; "John Addington Symonds once said to me"; "The Master of Balliol told me"—thus does she introduce her anecdotes. And you know those anecdotes that begin that way; me, I find them more efficacious than sheep-counting, rain on a tin roof, or alanol tablets. Just begin a story with such a phrase as "I remember Disraeli—poor old Dizzy!— once saying to me, in answer to my poke in the eye," and you will find me and Morpheus off in a corner, necking.

For brevity it would be hard to beat Alexander Woollcott's review of a show called *Wham!* His entire notice read: "Ouch!"

It was Woollcott who, after yet another disappointing evening at the theater, reported: "The audience strummed their

catarrhs." And taking a designer to task in another play he sin-
gled out one piece of furniture and observed, "The chair . . .
was upholstered in one of those flagrant chintzes, designed,
apparently, by the art editor of a seed catalogue."

Heywood Broun was one of the more down-to-earth of the Algonquin set. He greeted a new arrival on Broadway with the
sentence, "It opened at 8:40 sharp and closed at 10:40 dull."
And when the English actor Montague Love appeared in New
York, Broun summed up his performance with the observation,
"Mr. Love's idea of playing a he-man was to extend his chest
three inches and then follow it slowly across the stage."

When Walter Kerr went to see *Hook and Ladder* he concluded:
"It is the sort of play that gives failures a bad name." And on
the opening night of a new comedy, George S. Kaufman reported: "There was laughter at the back of the theater, leading
to the belief that someone was telling jokes back there."

Not all the Algonquins were negative. Franklin Pierce Adams
even enthused over actress Minnie Maddern Fiske in verse:

> Somewords she runstogether,
> Some others are distinctly stated.
> Somecometoofast and
>   s o m e t o o s l o w
> And some are $sy^nc_op^ated$.
> And yet no voice—I am sincere—
> Exists that I prefer to hear.

He was less charitable when he saw Helen Hayes as Cleopatra
in Bernard Shaw's play *Caesar and Cleopatra* in 1925. In his
review Adams remarked that it seemed as if the Egyptian
queen was suffering from "Fallen archness."

And in any Hall of Fame for acid criticism, there has to be a
special place for James Agee's verdict on the movie *Random
Harvest:* "I would like to recommend this film to those who
can stay interested in Ronald Colman's amnesia for two hours
and who could with pleasure eat a bowl of Yardley's shaving
soap before breakfast."

DICTIONARY WITH A DIFFERENCE

BIERCE MY HEART

A cynic is a blackguard who sees things as they are, and not as they ought to be.

So said Ambrose Gwinnet Bierce, a brilliant blackguard and a considerable wit, who was born on 24 June 1842 in Meigs County, Ohio. He was the son of a farmer and, since he never went to school, what education he got came from reading his father's books. When he left home he went to work for the Mint in San Francisco and began writing articles for local weeklies. In 1871 his first short story—"The Haunted Valley"— was published. On Christmas Day of that year he married and sailed for England, where he joined the staff of the journal *Fun* and began publishing humorous writings.

He was a very funny writer—a satirist in the tradition of Mark Twain—but not a happy man. In 1913, at the age of seventy-one, he left for Mexico "with a pretty definite purpose, which, however, is not at present disclosable." He was never heard from again, but his memorial remains in the form of his extraordinary *Devil's Dictionary*, a unique volume addressed to those "enlightened souls who prefer dry wines to sweet, sense to sentiment, and wit to humour."

I gave a generous sampling of Bierce's diabolical definitions in *The Joy of Lex*, and readers (well, two of them) cried out for more; so here are ten more gems from the prince of cynical lexicographers:

Altar n. They stood before the altar and supplied/
the fire themselves in which their fat was fried.

Brain, n. An apparatus with which we think that we think.

Cannon, n. An instrument employed in the rectification of national boundaries.

Debauchee, n. One who has so earnestly pursued pleasure that he has had the misfortune to overtake it.

Faith, n. Belief without evidence in what is told by one who speaks without knowledge, of things without parallel.

Genealogy, n. An account of one's descent from a man who did not particularly care to trace his own.

Marriage, n. The state or condition of a community consisting of a master, a mistress and two slaves, making in all two.

Patience, n. A minor form of despair, disguised as a virtue.

Philanthropist, n. A rich (and usually bald) old gentleman who has trained himself to grin while his conscience is picking his pocket.

Prejudice, n. A vagrant opinion without visible means of support.

BOWKER'S DOZEN

Gordon Bowker is a modern writer who has inherited Bierce's mantle of cynicism. Bowker's approach and tone are different from Bierce's, but some of his definitions are equally telling.

advertise   A form of prestidigitating by means of which a conjuror induces his audience to pick its own pocket under the impression that it is picking someone else's.

bigamy   A slip of the memory and the pen in the presence of the marriage register under the influence of matrimony.

body-builder   One who is fit for nothing.

celibate   A member of a union opposed to the union of members.

divorce   The stage of marriage at which sanity prevails.

drunk   A miracle worker who, while being unable to walk on water, is frequently to be seen staggering on whisky.

elitist   A humanist so inspired by the principle of equality that he strives to ensure that as many people as possible are equally deprived.

epitaph   An irritating reminder that someone else always has the last word.

freeloading   A quality of generosity that impels one human being to take the weight off another human being's feet by the simple device of taking the food off his plate.

gay   To be thoroughly bent on pleasure.

hangover   The mourning after the night before.

hooker   A fisher of men.

horoscope   A tale told by an idiot and believed by a fool.

Jello   An edible substance best comprehended as having the taste of a politician's promises and the consistency of his spine— sweet but nonexistent.

know-all   A benevolent ignoramus whose poverty of knowledge does not inhibit his generosity of mouth.

libel   A slip of the pen frequently precipitating a slip of the bank balance.

marxist   A prophet of doom who predicts the doom of profit.

moonie   A lune with a view.

orgy   A coming together of like-minded people.

pathologist   One who carves a good living out of a bad death.

psychiatry   The art of claiming to be able to cure those who are strung up practiced by one who deserves to be.

race course   Place where the rich get richer and the poor get excited.

salesman   A contortionist who puts his foot in your door, his tongue in your ear and his hand in your pocket while peddling.

shop steward   A benevolent soul who, being blind himself, is nevertheless prepared to lead others who are similarly stricken.

thief   A businessman who does not issue receipts.

tight   A condition of legless man and a garment of one-legged woman.

toy pistol   A gun-of-a-son.

E
ARTHQUAKE

Standing in line waiting to see the movie *Earthquake*, my verbivore friend Darryl Francis asked me: "How many other words end in *-quake*?"

Instantly I erupted with *moonquake* and *seaquake*, but that was it.

After the show I went home to consult *Webster's New International Dictionary* (second edition) and came up with a total of nine.

cowquake	Any of several grasses.
earthquake	A trembling of the earth.
heartquake	Fear or trepidation (an anagram of *earthquake*).
icequake	The crash attending the breaking up of ice masses.

seaquake	A seismic disturbance at sea.
statequake	A humorous term for a political upheavel in a state.
sunquake	A solar phenomenon like an earthquake.
waterquake	A disturbance of water by seismic action.
worldquake	A quake that shakes or affects the entire world.

Recuperating from the seismic shock of discovering that *cowquake* is a type of grass and not a bovine upheaval, I turned to the current unabridged *Webster's* and found these two *-quake* words:

aquake	Quaking.
moonquake	An agitation of the moon's surface that is analogous to a terrestrial earthquake.

Then I found that the 1976 Supplement to the *Oxford English Dictionary* has this to offer:

mirthquake	An entertainment that excites convulsive mirth.

A Dictionary of New English (by Barnhart, Steinmetz, and Barnhart) gave me a couple more.

starquake	A series of rapid changes in the shape of a star or in the distribution of its matter.
youthquake	The worldwide agitation caused by student uprisings and other expressions of rebellion among youth during the 1960s and 1970s.

And I was delighted to discover that in their *Second Barnhart Dictionary of New English,* the authors have uncovered an extra three:

corequake	A violent structural disruption in the core of a planet or star.
crustquake	A violent structural disruption in the crust of a planet or star.
Marsquake	A major seismic disturbance on the planet Mars.

When I got to seventeen *-quake* words I thought I'd reached the limit, but then Darryl sent me two press cuttings.

The first was from *Newsweek* and said of a particular earthquake: "It was not a superquake as earth tremors go." The other press report appeared in the London *Times* and gave names to the quakes occurring on the planets within the solar system:

> Marsquakes will be the first, then venusquakes and mercuryquakes, jupiterquakes, saturnquakes, uranusquakes, neptunequakes and plutoquakes. . . . And then the moons of these planets, Mars giving phobosquakes and deimosquakes, and Jupiter with its 12 satellites.

That makes a grand total of twenty-seven *quake* words. If you come across any others, do let me know. The effect could be cataclysmic.

FLEXILOQUENTLY SPEAKING

To me *flexiloquent* is one of the loveliest words in the English language, but back in 1678 a man called Phillips tried to get it banned. In his treatise *New World of Words* Phillips gave a list of words "to be used warily . . . or totally to be rejected as barbarous and illegally compounded or derived." These he regarded as "most notorious":

acetologous	logographer
acercecomie	lubidinity
alebromancy	lubrefaction
ambilogie	luctisonant
anopsie	miniography
aurigraphy	nihilification
circumbilivagination	nugipolyloquous

clemsonize	nugisonant
colligence	olfact
comprint	onologie
cynarctomachy	parvipension
effigiate	plastography
essentificate	plausidical
fallaciloquent	quadrigamist
flexiloquent	quadrisyllabous
helisphaerical	repatriation
hierogram	scelestick
holographical	solisequious
homologation	superficialize
horripilation	syllabize
humidiferous	synscentrick
illiquation	transpeciation
importous	tristitiation
imprescriptible	ultimity
incommiscibility	vaginipennous
indign	viscated
inimical	vulpinarity

Fortunately some of the words that offended Phillips have survived, among them:

agonize	ferocious
autograph	hagiography
bibliography	misanthropist
cacophony	misogynist
euthanasia	

Flexiloquent, meaning "speaking persuasively," definitely deserves to survive, and I am not alone in wanting to see (and hear) it brought back into general use.

Championing its cause, verbivore and crossword guru Roger Millington has launched an international campaign known as SUFF (Speak Up for Flexiloquent) on the grounds that we would all be better occupied reviving beautiful old words like *flexiloquent* than creating horrific new words and phrases like these:

kidvid	Children's television.
sciencing out	Removing defects from a product by scientific research.
sod poodles	Gun enthusiasts' name for prairie dogs.
wetware	Computer jargon for the human brain.

FLEXILOQUENT FAVORITES

Not long ago, on the night of April 3–4, 1982, I made my way into the *Guinness Book of World Records* when I got up and gave the longest-ever after-dinner speech. I talked nonstop for thirteen hours. It wasn't too difficult because I come from a family known for its verbosity.

As children my three sisters, my brother, and I were positively encouraged to speak in public by being taught a multitude of wonderful word games. These ten are my favorites and, often enough, they will help anyone speak with greater quick-wittedness, clarity, fluency, and flexiloquence.

BACKWARD SPELLING

The leader—self-appointed or chosen by popular acclaim—announces a word, and players must take it in turns to spell that word *backwards*. They have only ten seconds in which to do it, and so if they falter, fumble, or make a mistake, they drop out. The first player to spell the given word correctly and inside the time limit gains a point. The winner is the player with most points after a set number of words has been called.

COFFEEPOT

One of the players must block his ears while all the others choose a secret verb. When the verb's been chosen, the victim unblocks his ears and begins to question the others, substituting the word *coffeepot* for the mysterious verb. "How often do you coffeepot?" might be one question. "Can the over-eighties coffeepot with ease?" might be another. The victim is allowed ten questions, to which he must be given sensible replies and after which he must guess the identity of the secret verb. If he guesses correctly he gains a point and another player becomes the victim. The first player to score five points is the winner.

I PACKED MY BAG

This is the world-famous memory game in which the players have to keep track of an ever-lengthening list of items. The first player begins by saying. "I packed my bag, and in it I put my toothbrush." The second player then says, "I packed my bag, and in it I put my toothbrush and brown shoes." The third player continues, "I packed my bag, and in it I put my toothbrush, my brown shoes, and a copy of *The Joy of Lex*." And so it goes on around the group until someone forgets an item in the list or gets it in the wrong order, and then that player has to drop out and the others continue without him. The last player left packing his bag is the winner.

JUST A MINUTE

Players take it in turn to talk on a set subject for just a minute. They start with ten points apiece and when they have been talking for sixty seconds, without hesitating, repeating themselves, or deviating from the subject, they are awarded a further five points. However, if they *are* guilty of hesitation, repetition, or deviation they *lose* two points. Before the game starts an impartial observer should be chosen to choose the subjects, impose the penalties, and keep the score.

The more ridiculous the phrases the more entertaining the sixty seconds become. Almost anyone can talk about "Having a bath" for just a minute, but it is not so easy to keep going with topics like "Rat-catching in Oswego" and "I was a teenage taxidermist."

The last shall be first

A category is chosen—writers, rivers, cities, animals, scientists—and the players in turn call out words that fit the category, the catch being that the first letter of each word must be the same as the last letter of the preceding word. For example, if the category is countries, the words might be Australia, Austria, Aden, Norway, Yugoslavia, Afghanistan, Nigeria, and so on. Anyone who cannot think of a word drops out, and the last player left listing words correctly is the winner.

Messing about in quotes

One player comes up with a well-known phrase or quotation or cliché, and the other player has to suggest who might have said it. The players then swap roles. Nobody is awarded any points, penalties, or prizes, but with quick-witted players the game can be a joy. To set you going, who said, "Thank God it's Friday"? Why, Robinson Crusoe, of course!

The moulting ostrich

A leader is chosen and all he has to do is make the others smile or laugh. Grinning himself he says to each player in turn, "Alas, alas, my poor ostrich is moulting and I don't know what to do." To this each player must make a reasonable suggestion, keeping a totally straight face all the while. Anyone caught smiling, smirking, giggling, or busting into wild hysterics is disqualified.

When he goes around the second time the leader says, "Alas, alas, my poor ostrich is moulting, and I've got a boil on the end of my nose." For the third round he says, "Alas, alas, my poor ostrich is moulting, I've got a boil on the end of my nose, and my turkey's lost its stuffing." Anyone surviving all three rounds po-faced is a winner.

WHAT'S THE PROVERB

A victim is chosen and asked to cover his ears and eyes while the other players choose a secret proverb. They then tell the victim how many words the proverb contains, and he asks them each a question in an attempt to arrive at the proverb's identity. The victim gets his clues because the first player must include the first word of the proverb in his answer, the second player the second, the third the third, and so on until all the words in the proverb have been accounted for.

With "Too many cooks spoil the broth" as the secret proverb, the questioning might go something like this:

QUESTION:	Does this proverb express a basic truth about life?
ANSWER:	Yes, definitely. If anything, I'd say it's almost *too* true.
QUESTION:	Has it anything to do with love?
ANSWER:	*Many* proverbs have, but this one hasn't.
QUESTION:	Is it a sort of warning?
ANSWER:	You mean like "He who *cooks* the books ends up in jail"? Yes, I'd say it is.
QUESTION:	Is it a proverb about domestic life?
ANSWER:	Oh, I think it'd *spoil* the game if I gave you a straight answer to that.
QUESTION:	Is it an old proverb?
ANSWER:	*The* oldest I know.
QUESTION:	When did you first hear it?
ANSWER:	Years ago, when I was on holiday in Scotland, supping on *broth* and homemade bread, I was told it by a crofter's wife.

The questioner is allowed two questions for every word in the proverb and scores five points if he guesses it correctly when he has asked his allotted questions. At the end of a set number of rounds, the player with the highest score is the winner.

WORD LIGHTNING

The leader chooses a victim and gives him a letter. The hapless victim then has sixty seconds in which to rattle off as many words as he can that begin with the chosen letter. The leader keeps count. When all the players have been given a letter and a minute to do their best in, the player with the highest word count is the winner.

WORD ORDER

The first player calls out a word at random, the second player follows with another word suggested by the first word, the third player with another suggested by the second, and so on around the group. If the first word were *apple*, it might be followed by *pie, sky, blue, color, television, set, match, stick, cane, sugar,* and so on.

After a few rounds the first player suddenly shouts "Reverse order!" at which point the last player to speak must remember the word before his and all the words are repeated around the group in the reverse order—from *sugar* to *cane* to *stick* to *match* to *set* to *television* to *color* to *blue* to *sky* to *pie* to *apple*.

Anyone hesitating, getting the words in the wrong order, or forgetting a word loses a life. The player who has lost the least lives after five rounds is the winner.

G IRL TALK

Who said it?

    1 I don't mind living in a man's world as long as I can be a woman in it.
Brigitte Bardot or Marilyn Monroe?

    2 Whether women are better than men I cannot say—but I can say they are certainly no worse.
Golda Meir or Indira Gandhi?

    3 Women should remain at home, sit still, keep house, and bear and bring up children.
Martin Luther or Martin Luther King?

    4 Men seldom make passes at a girl who surpasses.
Franklin P. Jones or Dorothy Parker?

    5 Once made equal to man, woman becomes his superior.
Socrates or Germaine Greer?

6 There are no woman composers, never have been and possibly never will be.
Thomas Beecham or Thea Musgrave?

7 A science career for women is now almost as acceptable as being cheerleader.
Myra Barker or Farrah Fawcett?

8 Despite my thirty years of research into the feminine soul, I have not yet been able to answer . . . the great question that has never been answered: What does a woman want?
Sigmund Freud or Woody Allen?

9 The only question left to be settled now is, are women persons?
Twiggy or Susan B. Anthony?

10 Well, it's hard for a mere man to believe that woman doesn't have equal rights.
Dwight D. Eisenhower or Norman Mailer?

11 But if God had wanted us to think with our wombs, why did He give us a brain?
Erica Jong or Clare Boothe Luce?

12 It was either Isaac Newton or maybe it was Wayne Newton who once said, "A septic tank does not last forever." He was right.
Erma Bombeck or Kate Millett?

13 A suburban mother's role is to deliver children obstetrically once, and by car forever after.
Peter De Vries or Dr. Benjamin Spock?

14 When men reach their sixties and retire, they go to pieces. Women just go right on cooking.
Gail Sheehy or Betty Friedan?

15 Human beings are not animals, and I do not want to see sex and sexual differences treated as casually and amorally as dogs and other beasts treat them. I believe this could happen under the ERA.
Ronald Reagan or Phyllis Schlafly?

16 Woman's virtue is man's greatest invention.
Oscar Wilde or Cornelia Otis Skinner?

17 Fighting is essentially a masculine idea; a woman's weapon is her tongue.
Hermione Gingold or Rose Kennedy?

18 I'm a revolutionary—a revolutionary woman!
Mae West or Jane Fonda?

19 God made man, and then said I can do better than that and made woman.
Adela Rogers St. John or Billy Graham?

20 I feel very angry when I think of brilliant, or even interesting women whose minds are wasted on a home. Better have an affair. It isn't so permanent and you keep your job.
John Kenneth Galbraith or Burt Reynolds?

21 It's very difficult to run an army if the general is in love with the sergeant.
Margaret Mead or Col. George S. Patton III?

22 A liberated woman is one who feels confident in herself, and is happy in what she is doing. She is a person who has a sense of self. . . . It all comes down to freedom of choice.
Betty Ford or Billie Jean King?

23 There are two kinds of women: those who want power in the world, and those who want power in bed.
Jacqueline Kennedy Onassis or Zsa Zsa Gabor?

24 No one is born a woman.
Marilyn French or Simone de Beauvoir?

25 Women who insist upon having the same options as men would do well to consider the option of being the strong silent type.
Fran Lebowitz or Barbara Walters?

(See Answers.)

MISCELLANEOUS

If the U.S. Weather Bureau can break the habit of a lifetime and give hurricanes men's names, I think the rest of us should do our best to avoid sexist language as well. It's so ridiculous—and unnecessary—as these recent examples prove:

"The annual exhibition of the Society of Craftsmen—which includes women artists as well—opens on Thursday . . ."

". . . in terms even a housewife can understand."

"The Pap test, which has greatly reduced mortality from uterine cancer, is a boon to mankind."

"Judy Chicago will have her third one-man show this summer."

"It's the great secret of doctors, known only to their wives, that most ailments get better by themselves."

"What earthly purpose is served by tying a knot around your neck every day just so you can look like every other member of the species?"

"The average person (in one year) finds it no problem at all to have three head colds, one suburn, an attack of athlete's foot, twenty headaches, three hangovers, and five temper tantrums with adolescent children and still get in his sixty-one hours of shaving."

I know I should try to use nonsexist English and I do. But I don't know whether to use Ms. instead of Miss and Mrs. Opinions are still sharply divided:

> When you call me Miss or Mrs.
> You invade my private life,
> For it's not the public's business
> If I am, or was, a wife.

Others feel differently:

> In typing *Ms.* for *Mrs.*
> Your typewriter has slipped.
> I am a wife and mother,
> And not a manuscript.

Given that we all have first names, do we need titles at all? When you meet me in the street, you needn't bother with Mr. Just call me Gyles.

HIGH AND MIGHTY

TALK TALL

You will be familiar with tall stories, but you may not know
about tall *words*. Known as extenders, they are the ones in
which all the letters are written with extensions either above or
below the line. In handwriting and lowercase type, the extenders are *b, d, f, g, h, i, j, k, l, p, q, t,* and *y. Light* and *filthy* are
good examples of words made up exclusively of extenders. If
you want to talk tall, make sure your conversation is peppered
with tall words.

Here is a concise vocabulary of extenders for you to
master:

2 *letters:* by, hi, id, if, it

3 *letters:* bib, bid, bit, did, dig, dip, fib, fig, fit, fly, gig, hid, hip,
hit, ilk, ill, jib, kid, kip, kit, lid, lip, lit, pig, pip, pit, ply, thy, tip,
tit

   4 letters: bilk, bill, fill, flip, flit, gift, gild, glib, high, hill, hilt, idly, jilt, kill, kilt, lift, lilt, lily, pill, pith, tidy, till

   5 letters: biddy, billy, bitty, digit, ditty, fifth, fifty, fight, filth, giddy, glyph, hilly, idyll, kitty, light, piggy, pithy, thigh, tight

   6 letters: blight, fillip, flight, giggly, glibly, highly, plight, tidbit

The English language boasts hundreds of tall two-to-six-letter words but not many with seven letters or more. Here is the complete range:

   7 letters: bifidly, biggity, blighty, diglyph, fifthly, fittily, flighty, lightly, lithify, tightly, tiptilt

   8 letters: bifidity, filthify, libidibi, philippi

   9 letters: flightily, lilipilly

   10 letters: lillypilly

Anthropologists reckon that the world's tallest people are Australians, and so it's appropriate that *lillypilly,* the world's longest tallest word, should turn out to be a tall Australian tree with hard, fine-grained wood.

WEIGHTY WORDS

If each letter of the alphabet is given a weight—whether it's pounds, ounces, or kilograms—then every word in the language has a weight equal to the sum of the weights of the individual letters. Naturally the letter *A* should be given a weight of one unit, B two units, and so on through the alphabet, ending up with Z having a weight of twenty-six units.

   Obviously the lightest one-letter word is going to be the indefinite article *A,* but what is the lightest two-letter word? And what about longer words? I decided to search for the lightest words of all lengths up to fifteen letters. For each word in my list, I've given the total weight, the average weight per letter, and a brief definition. As might be expected, the average letter weight slowly increases with the length of the word, but there are occasional reversals.

   aa   (total weight = 2; average weight = 1.00) a type of volcanic lava.

baa	(4 and 1.33) a sheep's bleat.
abba	(6 and 1.50) a coarse fabric woven in the Middle East from wool.
caaba	(8 and 1.60) relating to the Islamic shrine at Mecca.
bacaba	(10 and 1.67) a palm, the fruits of which yield an oil used in soap manufacture.
cachaca	(20 and 2.86) white rum.
Fabaceae	(24 and 3.00) a family of plants that includes peas, beans, and various woody plants with pea-like flowers.
abdicable	(39 and 4.33) able to abdicate.
Galacaceae	(39 and 3.90) a family of herbs and shrubs.
cabbagehead	(39 and 3.55) a thick-witted person.
Baba-Abdallah	(47 and 3.92) a character in *The Arabian Nights*.
cabbageheaded	(48 and 3.69) stupid.
Hamamelidaceae	(81 and 5.79) a family of shrubs and trees comprising the witch hazels and related plants.
Coleochaetaceae	(102 and 6.80) a family of green algae.

The fourteen-letter specimen, *Hamamelidaceae*, is additionally interesting since it is the longest known word with all of its letters coming from the first half of the alphabet, *A* to *M*.

Having chased up fifteen lightweight words, I could hardly ignore the challenge of searching for fifteen heavyweight words—the words that have the greatest weights for each of the lengths up to fifteen letters. Here they are:

z	(total weight = 26; average weight = 26) something having the shape of the letter *z*.
wy	(48 and 24.00) something having the shape of the letter *y*.
zuz	(73 and 24.33) a silver coin of ancient Palestine.
zu-zu	(94 and 23.50) a soldier in the American Civil War.
wuzzy	(121 and 24.20) drunk.

xystus	(128 and 21.33) a tree-lined walk.
Zyzomys	(149 and 21.29) a genus of small Australian rodents.
untrusty	(158 and 19.75) not to be trusted.
Zorotypus	(175 and 19.44) a genus of insects.
tuzzymuzzy	(229 and 22.90) a garland of flowers.
trustworthy	(207 and 18.82) worthy of confidence.
untumultuous	(218 and 18.17) not turbulent.
untrustworthy	(242 and 18.61) not worthy of confidence.
tumultuousness	(240 and 17.14) commotion.
untrustworthily	(263 and 17.53) not in a trustworthy manner.

INTERNATIONAL SCRABBLE

I was in prison when I decided to launch the British National Scrabble Championships.

I wasn't an inmate, you understand. I was just visiting—doing research for a book about prisons—and I happened to notice a couple of jailbirds playing my favorite game. I already knew that Scrabble was the Royal Family's favorite board game, but I hadn't realized before that its popularity was so universal: that it could delight not just Her Majesty but even those detained in her prisons at her pleasure. There and then I decided that any game that had such a breadth of appeal had to have its own national tournament.

Of all the labels that have been attached to me since I launched the first Scrabble Championship back in 1971—"Scrabble King," "Scrabble Guru," "Mr. Scrabble"—the one I treasure most appeared in a newspaper noted for its inspired misprints. "Mr. Gyles Brandreth," it said, "is the founder and organiser of the National Rabble Championships."

Let me say at once that there are no more civilized people on the planet than Scrabble players, but it can't be denied that passions *do* get aroused from time to time. As the poet—in this case, demented Scrabbler Robin Anderson—puts it so perfectly in his "Ode to Scrabble":

Where double beats treble but triple beats all
But you may have to settle for nothing at all
And chuck in your letters
And grope for their betters
And bring out a handful still worse than before:
Where your noun if deemed proper
Will bring you a cropper
And a cheat is worth more than playing fair
Where with just one *E* more
You've a staggering score
And your word may be rude—you don't care:
You are plotting and scheming, quixotically dreaming
Of clearing your tray and going out
But the next player's eyed
The place you had espied
And your staggering score's up the spout;
So you spring from your chair
Raise the board in the air
And smash it down hard round his ears—
Other players are crying
The letters are flying:
You're charged and end up with three years.
If your nerves are not icy, your temper is dicey,
When losing, you tear out your hair;
If you can't keep your cool
Then follow the rule—
When you dabble with Scrabble, beware!

Among the countries that hold national Scrabble championships in English are Singapore and the United Kingdom.

Both use *Chambers Twentieth Century Dictionary* as their reference when a word is in dispute, though each places different limitations upon the type of word permitted. For example, Scottish words are not valid in Singapore although they frequently appear on U.K. Scrabble boards. Some of these same words of Scottish origin *are* valid in the United States provided that they also appear in *The Official Scrabble Players Dictionary*. The OSPD is the reference used in official American competitions with the result that the United Kingdom and the United States will, sometimes, be at variance over which words are or are not valid for competitive Scrabble.

To illustrate that often-entertaining difference, here are half a dozen puzzles based upon various games of Scrabble at various stages in play. At the point at which the puzzle begins, all words on the board are valid in both the United Kingdom and the United States and you are given a rack of seven tiles to play.

It's your move and the challenge is to use your tiles to achieve the highest possible score—using either British words or American words or both.

Puzzles begin on the following page.

AEEGLRS

AEELRST

AADOPRX

OGJOQWZ

AAIJNRZ

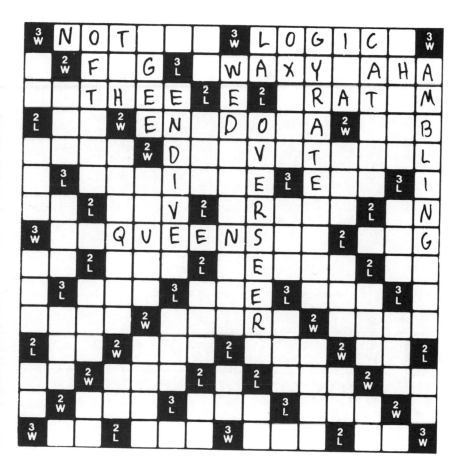

ABGILOO

(NOTE: the G in AMBLING is a blank tile.)

(See Answers.)

J ARGON FOR BEGINNERS

BUREAUCRATESE

You will be relieved to hear that the Reagan administration is as determined to eradicate gobbledygook as was its predecessor. In *The Joy of Lex* I quoted the White House lawyer who apologized to President Carter for producing an incomprehensible piece of legalese and then said: "I see your point, Mr. President. I had better laymanize the whole thing."

Now Malcolm Baldridge, President Reagan's Secretary for Commerce, has started admonishing his staff for their overblown use of English. Secretary Baldridge wants his officials to adopt a concise style that is "halfway between Zane Grey and Ernest Hemingway."

The prospect of government documents written in a kind of English that's both Grey and Earnest may not be that appetizing, but it can only be an improvement on the bureaucratese that is the order of the day at present. At this moment in time—if you'll pardon the expression—we are still being fed incomprehensible gobbledygook like this:

> Any employee whose current salary rate exceeds the new top of the salary range for his or her classification will not be eligible for the general increase unless the new top of the salary range for his or her classification exceeds the employee's current salary rate.

> Component corporations of component corporations—If a corporation is a component corporation of an acquiring corporation, under subsection (b) or under this subsection, it shall (except for the purposes of section 742d and section 743a) also be a component corporation of the corporation of which such acquiring corporation is a component corporation.

> Apparatus for removing casings from sausages and the like (U.S. Patent No.2,673,646)
> In a sausage-skinning machine, means for rotating a sausage about its longitudinal axis, means for simultaneously holding a part of the skin against rotative movement with the sausage to cause said skin to be torn off said sausage circumferentially, and means for simultaneously removing said sausage endwise with respect to said holding means, said rotating, holding and moving means being operatively related to one another to cause said skin to be torn off and stripped from the sausage helically.

The Occupational and Safety Health Administration Rulebook defines "an exit" as:

> . . . that portion of a means of egress which is separated from all other spaces of the building or structure by construction or equipment as required in this subpart to provide a protected way of travel to the exit discharge.

And "a means of egress" as:

> . . . a continuous and unobstructed way of exit travel from any point in a building or structure to a public way and consists of three separate and distinct parts: the way of exit access, the exit and the way of exit discharge.

American bureaucrats aren't the only guilty ones. My Gobbledygook Award for 1982 goes to the Indian civil servant who concocted this paragraph for the prospectus of the Central Institute of Hindi in Delhi:

NATURE OF COURSE:

Unlike language courses in the universities which are content oriented, the Institute offers its courses with a functional approach to the study of language. As it believes in the priority of approach over method and in turn of method over technique, the courses in Hindi as an other tongue have been evolved on the basis of different roles a language plays in a speech community i.e. auxiliary, supplementary, complementary or equative. Instead of holding in the most inflexible form of stimulus-response formulation in terms of behavioristic tenor, care has been taken in developing the course in direction of imparting language skills creatively in consonance with the psychological, cultural and social rules of Hindi speech community. The Institute has also evolved its functional approach of language analysis in order to resolve the basic contradictions between grammar and usage.

COMMERCIALESE

Understanding the jargon of the worlds of business and commerce isn't easy, but if you want to get to the top you need to know what your colleagues—and your rivals—are talking about. To help you gain a better understanding of contemporary commercialese, here is a glossary of some useful words and phrases:

Activate. To make carbons and add more names to the memo.

Advanced design. Beyond the comprehension of the ad agency's copywriters.

All new. Parts not interchangeable with existing models.

Approved, subject to comment. Redraw the damned thing.

Automatic. That which you can't repair yourself.

Channels. The trail left by interoffice memos.

Clarify, to. To fill in the background with so many details that the foreground goes underground.

Conference. A place where conversation is substituted for the dreariness of labor and the loneliness of thought.

Confidential memorandum. No time to mimeograph/photocopy for the whole office.

Consultant. Someone who borrows your watch to tell you what time it is—then walks away with the watch.

Coordinator. The person who has a desk between two expediters (see *expedite*).

Developed after years of intensive research. Discovered by accident.

Expedite. To confound confusion with commotion.

Forwarded for your consideration. You hold the bag for a while.

Give someone the picture, to. To make a long, confused, and inaccurate statement to a newcomer.

Give us the benefit of your present thinking. We'll listen to what you have to say as long as it doesn't interfere with what we've already decided to do.

In conference. Nobody can find him/her.

In due course. Never.

Infrastructure. (1) The structure within an infra. (2) The structure outside the infra. (3) A building with built-in infras.

It is in process. So wrapped up in red tape that the situation is almost hopeless.

Let's get together on this. I'm assuming you're as confused as I am.

Note and initial. Let's spread the responsibility for this.

Policy. We can hide behind this.

Program A. Any assignment that cannot be completed by one telephone call.

See me. Come down to my office, I'm lonely.

Sources. Reliable source—the person you just met. Informed source—the person who told the person you just met. Unimpeachable source—the person who started the rumor originally.

Top priority. It may be idiotic, but the boss wants it.

Under active consideration. We're looking in the files for it.

We are making a survey. We need more time to think of an answer.

We will look into it. By the time the wheel makes a full turn, we assume you will have forgotten about it too.

STYLESPEAK

You can be wearing all the right clothes, you can be seen in all the right places, but if your conversation doesn't have the right ring to it, everyone will know you're neither a real lady nor a true gentleman.

If you want to impress the world at large with your high social standing, your vocabulary has got to include all the classiest words and phrases. Here they are:

awesome Terrific, great.

big fella Affectionate name used by men with and to each other.

big guy Same as above.

blow away, to To impress, overwhelm.

blown out Wasted, tired, hung over.

brothel stompers Suede shoes.

chew face Kiss.

classic Event, person, object, or social gathering that is different or strange.

cute Supreme accolade.

darling Synonymous with *cute*.

dorky Clumsy, ignorant of style, what most of us are trying not to be.

eat my shorts Go jump in the lake.

excellent A good idea.

flamer Faux pas, and the perpetrator of the same.

get Chinese, to Getting really stoned.

gross Disgusting.

heavy . . . action Whatever one does a lot.

hoot That which is amusing.

how arch Inappropriate.

how, (to) A cry of derision, to make fun of.

in a big way An intensifier, as in: "I got crocked in a big way."

intense Anything really fun.

jacked out Angry.

lame Weak, pathetic.

lunch, to To meet for midday meal.

major Signifying large quantities of anything being done in a big way.

must Something you have to have.

neat Something cute, but not as cute as *cute*.

need a foghorn To be confused or unaware.

nice Not nice, awful.

on fire When you've made a social gaffe, you're on fire.

outrageous Lively, funny, or memorable.

outstanding Synonymous with *excellent*, but more so.

out to lunch Confused or unaware.

panic Something or someone hysterically funny.

psyched Psychologically predisposed, enthusiastic, brainwashed, ready.

really Universal term of agreement and emphasis.

rettes Cigarettes.

rude In bad taste, gauche, bad.

scoots Dollars.

shoe Top draw; very acceptable.

skied Psyched, as in "I'm ready for the challenge."

smash mouth, to To kiss.

spaced Head in the clouds.

stitch Someone or something funny.

stitches The state you're in when you find something funny.

sucked Disappointing.

super Good (with reference to an experience).

talent Boyfriend or girlfriend.

to die (adj.) Wonderful, fantastic.

too much Amusing, fun-loving.

to the max All the way.

trash To goof, make fun.

tuna Either steady girlfriend or recent acquisition.

unreal Pleasant, enjoyable.

walk on Get lost.

wild Dirty, dangerous, or inclined toward wearing a lot of black.

zoned Blitzed, exhausted, burned out.

PREPTALK

According to the social climber's bible, *The Official Preppy Handbook,* "Preppies would rather take it easy. They'd prefer not to expend energy speaking. For the sake of basking in their own ingenuity as well as camaraderie, they've developed a codified set of abbreviations which cut conversation time to a minimum while insuring that non-Preps will have no idea what or who is being discussed."

By definition my readers must belong to the upper classes, and so none of them will have any difficulty working out what each of these twenty sets of initials stands for:

A.T.D.	O.O.C.
B.M.O.C.	O.T.W.
C.B.C.	P.D.A.
F.T.P.	R & I
G & T	S.A.
H²	S.O.T.
H.T.H.	T.B.A.
I.B.M.	T.D.C.
N.O.C.D.	T.T.F.W.
N.T.B.	U.R.L.

(See Answers.)

KARAT SOUP

CHAUVINISM FOR BEGINNERS

Sometimes the English used by English-speaking people makes me despair. Then I go abroad on vacation and discover that the English used by non-English–speaking people is even worse. On my travels I have collected examples of "foreigner's English" from all over the world. Here are the best—or worst:

> By order of the police, one obliges the frequenters of the Camping to are wearing bath-costumes that are not giving offence to the morals. (Notice in campsite in Italy)

> It is forbidden to steal hotel towels please. If you are not to do such is please not to read notis. (Notice in Tokyo hotel)

> Persons are requested not to occupy seats in this café without consummation. (Notice in French café)

In case of fire please do your utmost to alarm the hall porter. (Notice in Austrian hotel)

Visitors are requested not to throw coffee or other matter into the basin. Why else it stuffs the place inconvenient for the other world. (Notice in an Italian hotel)

What you must not do

To walk around alone or in groups, in an inadequate form and adapting attitudes that denote a personal bad state, to offend the elemental conduct.

To make noises and scandals in the sight of the public and establishments.

Sit down or lie down in sight of the public, to obstruct the freedom of the people.

Utilizing ponds, fountains, for personal use.

To break or tear objects in the sight of the public or crowded places.

To utilize percussion instruments after midnight. (Notice from festival in Pamplona, Spain)

Gerona. Here is a name and a symbol. A name set in the tentacles of Empire. Of aristocratic craddle. Old and fruitful savour, speaking about daring legions, unfinishing ways, aqueducts, warlike marching and toges. Gerona was promise and reality. Promise because upon it would fall the evangelic seed of the mustard, not because less strong in aborescence and the fruit. (From a guidebook to Gerona, Spain)

To remember of this period are the failed lading of the French revolutionaries on the northern coast of the island (1793), the uprising of 1795, the consequent march of the judge C. M. Angioi on Cagliari, thwarted off Oristano in 1796 and the attempt also fruitless of the notary Cilocca in 1802. (From a guidebook to Sardinia)

Although every possible care has been taken, I do not accept responsibility for inoccurancies. (From a guidebook to Malta)

Translation Please

Foreigners' English may be bad at times, but the way English-speaking people speak other languages is almost invariably worse. Here is a glossary of words and phrases in French, German, Arabic, Spanish, Italian, and Latin, with a selection of translations supplied by American high-school students:

abito	A piece of.
affaire de coeur	Pigeon bazaar.
ahorros	Four-legged animal used for racing.
à la carte	Served from the trolley.
à la russe	In a hurry.
amour propre	Dock pile.
Angebot	To wait, loiter.
apenas	Joy, pleasure.
apéritif	Dentures.
arriba	Large stream.
Auspuff	Cobweb duster.
bacchich	Backache.
bagatelle	Talkative females.
baroque	Short of money.
beau geste	Big joke.
bonis avibus	Free ride on public transport.
billet	Academic qualification.
bord de la route	Soliciting hitchhiker.
brouhaha	French joy of cooking.
brefs	Pants.
café Nero	Coffee served with brandy on the surface.
campagna	Italian girlfriend.
ça ne fait rien	Good weather.
carte blanche	Hospital trolley.
château	French conversation.
cortège	Small house in the country.

coup de cheveaux	Horse race.
crèche	Sound of breaking crockery.
cul-de-sac	Out of the bag.
damnosa	Very inquisitive.
de gustibus	Very windy.
déjeuner	Travel.
de mal en pis	Urgent need to pass water.
de optimo maximo	Very good eyesight.
déshabiller	To kick the habit.
emeraudes	Piles.
en ami	Hostile person.
esprit de corps	Liquor served in military messes.
extrados	More, please.
farceur	Comic play.
farci	Farce.
fiasco	Italian wine bottle.
flèche	Skin.
fruits de mer	Sea weed.
gendarme	Strong arm of the law.
grande dame	Fat lady.
grand prix	Large reward.
hasta la vista	You have nice views.
homme d'affaires	Libertine.
hors de combat	Dog fight.
imo pectore	He kissed her.
in toto	Wearing a ballet skirt.
infra dig	Archaeologist.
in loco parentis	In one's parent's train.
in statu pupillari	Contact lens.
inter alia	Domestic flights.
intermezzo	Between meals.
intime	At the right moment.
jus contra bellum	I am overweight.

juste milieu	Just a minute!
karat	Vegetable.
kip	Chicken,
kipper	Small chicken.
laissez-faire	Idle woman.
lapsus memoriae	Poor memory.
largo	Italian beer.
legato	Tailor's measurement.
lemma	Fruit drink.
libido	Bathroom fitting.
libretto	Type of sandal.
langua franca	Speaking your mind.
l'état c'est moi	I am in a state.
ma foi	My liver.
maladie	Madam.
mal vu	Poor eyesight.
mauvais goût	Swollen leg.
mis en page	Slip of the pen.
mistral	Folk singer.
negligé	Careless.
n'importe	There is no port left.
noblesse oblige	Nobody will help.
nom de plume	Quill pen.
non compos mentis	Nonbiodegradable.
nota bene	Potato, or cabbage.
nouvelle vague	Modern novel.
oeil-de-boeuf	Oxtail soup.
obscurum per obscuris	You're standing in front of the light.
odium	A drug.
odium theologicum	Incense.
palomine	Friend of mine.
par excellence	Very good father.
pas de deux	Father of twins.

passé	Father has spoken.
pax vobiscum	Expression used by Italian waiters when tipping peas into your lap.
pizzicato	Italian take-out.
polonaise	Hay fever.
post-obitum	Earth re-entry.
presto	Tight shoe.
rechauffé	Rearrange.
rentier	Pay money to landlord.
semper paratus	Always a parrot.
son et lumière	Your son is smoking.
sotto voce	Slurred speech.
sub poena	Under the pony.
table d'hôte	Hot plate.
terra cotta	Fear of beds.
terra incognita	Fear of the unknown.
tour de force	Troop inspection.
tour de main	Palmistry.
vice versa	Limerick.
vis-à-vis	To return the insult.
volta face	Wooden horse.
zweifellos	Two men.

BON MOT

I think the last word on the subject belongs to Goethe: "Wer fremde Sprachen nicht kennt, weiss nichts von seiner eigenen."

How true.

LOVE, LOVE, LOVE!

They say it's love that makes the world go round. They also say that variety is the spice of life. On both counts I agree with them. I never tire of hearing the words "I love you," but now and again I do like to be offered a variation on the theme. Here, drawn from real life and the movies, are the eight most stirring declarations of love I know of:

"I have seen only you, I have admired only you, I desire only you."
—Napoleon Bonaparte to Marie Walewska

"I was born when you kissed me, I died when you left me. I lived a few days when you loved me."
—Gloria Grahame to Humphrey Bogart in *In a Lonely Place*

"I love you soulfully and bodyfully, properly and improperly, every way that a woman can be loved."
—George Bernard Shaw to English actress Ellen Terry, with whom he had an epistolary romance

"I cannot live without my life . . . I cannot love without my soul. . . ."
—Laurence Olivier as Heathcliff after the death of Cathy in *Wuthering Heights*

"In thy face I have seen the eternal."
—Baron Christian von Bunsen to his wife as he lay dying

"Oh my Lolita! . . . a ray of sunshine at the break of day! As a stream of light in an obscure night."
—No, not Nabokov, but Ludwig I of Bavaria to the dancer, Lola Montez

"I need your love as a touchstone of my existence. It is the sun which breathes life into me."
—Juliette Drouet to her lover Victor Hugo

"Don't ever think of the things you can't give me—You've trusted me with the dearest heart of all—and it's so damn much more than anybody else in all the world has ever had."
—Zelda Sayre to F. Scott Fitzgerald

Power for lust

Perhaps people with a lust for power are more passionate than the rest of us. Certainly, for highly charged love letters, it would be hard to top these three—from Winston Churchill, Napoleon Bonaparte, and Eva Peron.

WINSTON CHURCHILL TO HIS WIFE, CLEMENTINE

France
September, 1919

My darling one
    Only these few lines to mark the eleventime we have seen

the 12th Sept. together. How I rejoice to think of my gt good fortune on that day! There came to me the greatest happiness and the greatest honour of my life. . . .

My dear it is a rock of comfort to have yr love and companionship at my side. Every year we have formed more bonds of deep affection. . . .

I can never express my gratitude to you for all you have done for me and for all you have been to me.

Yr ever loving and devoted
W.

NAPOLEON BONAPARTE TO JOSEPHINE BEAUHARNAIS

February 1796
Seven o'clock in the morning

My waking thoughts are all of you. Your portrait and the remembrance of last night's delirium have robbed my sense of repose. Sweet and incomparable Josephine, what an extraordinary influence you have over my heart. Are you vexed? Do I see you sad? Are you ill at ease? My soul is broken with grief and there is no rest for your lover. . . .

But is there more for me when, delivering ourselves up to the deep feelings which master me, I breathe out upon your lips, upon your heart, a flame which burns me up? Ah! It was this past night I realised that your portrait was not you.

You start at noon. I shall see you in three hours. Meanwhile, mio dolce amor, accept a thousand kisses, but give me none, for they fire my blood.

EVA PERON TO HER HUSBAND, JUAN:

Flying to Europe
June 6th, 1947

I am very sad to be leaving because I am unable to live away from you, I love you so much that what I feel for you is a kind of idolatory, perhaps I don't know how to show what I feel for you, but I assure you that I fought very hard in my life with the ambition to be someone and I suffered a great deal.

But then you came and made me so happy that I thought it was a dream and since I had nothing else to offer you but my heart and my soul I gave them to you wholly but in all these three years of happiness, greater each day, I never ceased to adore you for a single hour or thank Heaven for the goodness of God in giving me this reward of your love, and I tried at all times to deserve it by making you happy.

I don't know if I achieved that, but I can assure you that nobody has ever loved or respected you more than I have.

I am so faithful to you that if God wished me not to have you in this happiness and took me away I would still be faithful to you in my death and adore you from the skies. . . .

Many kisses, but many kisses. . ·. .

Evita.

THE BROWNING VERSION

Some of the finest poetry in the English language has love as its central theme. Of all the great love poems my favorite is one of Elizabeth Barrett Browning's *Sonnets from the Portuguese:*

How do I love thee? Let me count the ways.
I love thee to the depth and breadth and height
My soul can reach, when feeling out of sight
For the ends of Being and ideal Grace.
I love thee to the level of every day's
Most quiet need, by sun and candle light.
I love thee freely, as men strive for Right;
I love thee purely, as they turn from Praise.
I love thee with the passion put to use
In my old griefs, and with my childhood's faith.
I love thee with a love I seemed to lose
With my lost saints—I love thee with the breath,
Smiles, tears, of all my life!—and, if God choose,
I shall but love thee better after death.

BITTERSWEET

I am a sentimentalist. I like my love poetry sickly sweet. A verse, like this one sent by Dorothy Parker to her husband who was fighting in the 1914/18 War, I find almost too painful to bear.

Only, for the nights that were,
Soldier, and the dawns that came,
When in sleep you turn to her,
Call her by my name.

LOVE AND MARRIAGE

Not all the poets who have celebrated love and marriage in
their work have taken the subject as seriously or as sneeringly
as did Mrs. Browning or Mrs. Parker. Look at these five verses,
all written by men:

I recollect a nurse called Ann,
Who carried me about the grass,
And one fine day a fine young man
Came up, and kissed the pretty lass.
She did not make the least objection!
Thinks I "Aha!
When I can talk I'll tell Mama,"
    And that's my earliest recollection.
                        FREDERICK LOCKER-LAMPSON

When I was young and full of life
I loved the local doctor's wife,
And ate an apple every day
To keep the doctor far away.
                        THOMAS LAMONT

'Twas in a restaurant they met,
Romeo and Juliet
He had no cash to pay the debt,
So Romeo'd while Juliet.
                        VERNON NAISMITH

"Come, come," said Tom's father, "At your
        time of life,
There's no longer excuse for thus playing the rake—
It is time you should think, boy, of taking a wife."
"Why, so it is, father—whose wife shall I take?"
                        THOMAS MOORE

I have come to the conclusion
Having given it a test,
That of all my wife's relations,
I like myself the best.

HENRY ROBINSON

LOVE ALL

Of all the great screen lovers, the greatest was undoubtedly Groucho Marx. Who could fail to be bowled over by lines like these?

"Send two dozen roses to Room 424 and put 'Emily I love you' on the back of the bill."

"Emily will you marry me—I will never look at another horse."

MERRY CHRISTMAS

There's always been a Christmas.

That's not quite true. There's *almost* always been a Christmas. Certainly there was one long before Christ was born, though it wasn't called Christmas then. The deep midwinter has been a time for jollification and celebration for thousands of years, and even if Adam and Eve didn't hang out stockings in the Garden of Eden, many of the Christmas traditions we now take for granted began not so long after the Fall.

The Ancient Romans launched their week-long celebration of fire and light, the Saturnalia, on December 17 and quickly followed it up with three days of New Year festivities, called Kalends. In between, on December 25 itself, came the *Dies Natalis Invicti Solis*—the Birthday of the Unconquered Sun—sacred to Mithras, god of light, and to Attis, the Phrygian sun-god.

These Roman holidays may sound staid, but by all accounts the Saturnalia was a time when the Latins really let their hair down. It wasn't simply an excuse for indulging in the pleasures of wine, women, and song; it was also an opportunity for organized anarchy. Servants dressed up as their masters, lords pretended to be slaves, gentlemen danced drunkenly in the streets wearing little but blackened faces and animal skins. On a gentler level, special lamps were burned, special greenery was brought in to decorate the home, and special presents were exchanged.

The lights, the evergreens, and the gifts were also a feature of another pre-Christian midwinter romp: The Festival of Yule. On December 22, the time of the winter solstice when the sun is farthest from the Equator and at the point where it appears to pause before returning, the old Norsemen lit giant fires to the grim gods Odin and Thor, ate too much, drank too much, and wished one another a Very Merry Yuletide.

They weren't the only ones to use the winter solstice as a peg for a pagan party. The Druids chose the day for celebrating the Festival of Nolagh. The Greeks latched on to it as the birthday of Ceres, Hercules, and Bacchus. The Egyptians claimed it as the feast day of Horus, the son of Isis. And the list could go on and on because quite some time before the Christians decided that December 25 should be the birthday of Jesus, people from all over the world—from Greece and Rome, from Scandinavia and the Middle East, from India and China and South America—all had their own particular festivities at this time of year.

In fact, when Pope Julius I decided around the year 350 that Jesus' birthday should no longer be on January 1 or March 29 or September 29 but on December 25, he happily chose a date that had always been associated with merrymaking. And, with a bit of luck, it always will be.

The meaning of Christmas

The history of Christmas apart, do you know its true meaning? Now that I've checked it out in every dictionary in the Library of Congress, I do. There's more to the word than you'd imagine. According to a wide range of reliable authorities, Christmas is:

1 an annual church festival kept on December 25 or by the Armenians on January 6 in memory of the birth of Christ, celebrated generally by a particular church service, special gifts and greetings, and observed in most Christian communities as a legal holiday.

2 any similar festivity or revelry.

3 the Christmas season.

4 the festival season from Christmas Eve till after New Year's or (especially in England) till Epiphany.

5 Christmas Day, December 25.

6 the Christmas holidays.

7 something connected with the celebration of Christmas, as a gift.

8 any gift or present bestowed at Christmastime.

9 Christmas decorations.

10 evergreens used for decorations at Christmas, as the European holly.

11 the holly, *Ilex aquifolium.*

12 something special to drink at Christmastime.

13 a Texan term for whiskey.

14 a cake made on Christmas Eve.

15 any ostentatious display, as of clothing, jewelry, etc.

16 a garish article of clothing or jewelry, or one that sparkles.

17 a shower of metallic foil dropped by an airplane or released from an artillery shell to jam enemy radar or communications systems.

18 a mild, euphemistic expletive.

19 payday.

20 a baptismal name, now uncommon as a boy's name and practically unknown as a girl's.

21 a frequent surname for one born near Christmas.

22 the surname of Gerard Christmas, an English carver who died in 1634.

23 the surname of Henry Christmas, an English writer who lived from 1811 until 1868.

24 a surname that appears over forty times in the London telephone directory.

25 a town in Gila County, Arizona.

26 a town in Orange County, Florida.

27 a town in Alger County, Michigan.

28 a lake in Hennepin County, Minnesota.

29 a place in Bolivar County, Mississippi.

30 a town in Morgan County, Tennessee.

31 a mountain in the Antarctic, at 82 degrees south, 159 degrees east.

32 a British island in the Indian Ocean about 190 miles south of Java.

33 one of the Line Islands in the central Pacific Ocean south of Hawaii, being the largest atoll in the Pacific.

34 a verb meaning "to celebrate Christmas."

35 an obsolete verb meaning "to provide with Christmas cheer."

36 a verb meaning "to decorate with evergreens for Christmas."

37 a verb meaning "to sell Christmas decorations."

38 a verb meaning "to adorn with Christmas decorations."

39 a verb meaning "to spend Christmas."

40 a verb, short for *Christmas Eve,* that is rhyming slang for "to believe."

41 a verb meaning "to engage in sexual activity."

So now you know what it's all about, have a cool Yule.

NEVER SAY DIE

Never say die if you've got more than one of them. *Dice* is the plural of *die*.

The English language is rich in curious words that have even curiouser plurals. Here's an A to Z of some of them. They can all be found in *Webster's Third New International Dictionary:*

SINGULAR	PLURAL
Adai	Adaize
brother	brethren
Chetty	Chettyars
Dukhobor	Dukhobortsky
englyn	englynion
Feis	Feiseanna
goosefoot	goosefoots

holluschick	holluschickie
iter	intinera
juger	jugera
Kuvasz	Kuvaszok
landsman	landsleit
mongoose	mongooses
never-was	never-weres
ornis	ornithes
paries	parietes
quadrans	quadrantes
rubai	rubaiyat
shtetl	shtetlach
tenderfoot	tenderfoots
ulcus	ulcera
vila	vily
wunderkind	wunderkinder
Xhosa	Amaxhosa
yad	yadayim
zecchino	zecchini

Having given you twenty-six curious plurals each beginning with a different letter of the alphabet, let me give you another twenty-six, each *ending* with a different letter of the alphabet.

SINGULAR	PLURAL
vas	vasa
chub	chub
calpul	calpullec
squid	squid
bildungsroman	bildungsromane
riff	riff
hog	hog
matzo	matzoth
jajman	jajmani
Bhumij	Bhumij

puli	pulik
court-martial	courts-martial
seraph	seraphim
torte	torten
buffalo	buffalo
sheep	sheep
Qaraqalpaq	Qaraqalpaq
krone	kroner
plural	plurals
matzo	matzot
ushabti	ushabtiu
Pshav	Pshav
mother-in-law	mothers-in-law
plateau	plateaux
pince-nez	pince-nez

SINGULAR QUIZ

Here are twenty-five everyday words. Can you give the plural for each of them?

1 ax
2 ox
3 son-in-law
4 potato
5 piccolo
6 attorney general
7 lieutenant colonel
8 opus
9 index
10 teaspoonful
11 mister
12 man-of-war
13 manservant

14 oboe
15 cherub
16 crisis
17 datum
18 cannon
19 addendum
20 agenda
21 phenomenon
22 madam
23 pelvis
24 paymaster general
25 brigadier general

(See Answers.)

O LL KORRECT, OK?

Too much nonsense has been talked about the expression *OK*. I'm here to set the record straight, and I intend to be quick about it. OK?

OK does *not* come from the Choctaw word *oke* meaning "it is" or from *hoke* meaning "yes."

OK does *not* come from the practice of grading words for furniture making, the best oak of course being *Oak A*.

OK does *not* come from the O.K. Club named after Old Kinderhook, Martin Van Buren's birthplace.

OK, are you ready for the truth? In New England 150 or so years ago there was a craze for abbreviations, and *OK* and *O.K.* first appeared in print in various Boston newspapers, along with many other abbreviations. *R.T.B.S.* was "remains to be seen." *S.P.* was "small potatoes." *O.F.M.* was "our first men." Inevitably a number of the abbreviations had to be explained for the benefit of uninitiated readers. E.g., the *Boston Morning Post* of June 12, 1838, spoke of "a duel W.O.O.O.F.C. (with one of our first citizens)." The craze went so far as to produce abbreviations of intentional misspellings. *N.G.* for "no go" and *A.R.* for "all right" gave way to *K.G.* for "know go," and *O.W.* for "oll wright." *O.K.* for "oll korrect" followed quite naturally. And of all the varied and colorful abbreviations and misspellings of the time, however, it alone spread and survived.

So now you know, OK?

P
ARDON ME!

My mistake

Mrs. Beverly Nina Avery, of Los Angeles, California, has been divorced sixteen times . . . the Decca recording company said "No" to the Beatles because they thought they were too old-fashioned . . . Demolition experts in Baltimore, Maryland, recently razed a two-story house to the ground and then discovered it was the wrong one . . . *The New York Times* once ran a headline that read "Judge Acts to Keep Theater Open" . . . and not long ago I came across this inscription on a tombstone:

Sacred to the memory of
MAJOR JAMES BRUSH
who was killed by
the
accidental discharge
of a pistol by
his orderly
14th of April 1831.
Well done thou good and
faithful servant.

Like it or not, believe it or not, we all make mistakes. Indeed, mistake-making is one of the very few factors that can honestly be said to unite mankind.

As a writer prone to making mistakes, I'm in excellent company. There have been not-so-deliberate slips in some of the greatest masterpieces of world literature. For example, in Daniel Defoe's novel *Robinson Crusoe* the shipwrecked hero decides to salvage some goods from his ship before it sinks completely. Defoe describes how Crusoe removes all his clothes before swimming to the ship, but forgetting this fact he allows him to fill his pockets with biscuits once he is on board!

And Sir Arthur Conan Doyle gave Sherlock Holmes's sidekick, Dr. Watson, one war wound—but in two places. In *A Study in Scarlet* the wound is in the shoulder, while in *The Sign of Four* it is in Watson's leg.

In case you want to assess your own capacity for spotting unlikely errors, I have devised a quick quiz to help you.

1 Copy down the following: A bird in
in the hand is worth two in the bush.

2 Which is correct: Nine and five are thirteen or nine and five is thirteen?

3 Can you spot any mistakes in these famous quotations?
a. When Winter comes, is Spring not far behind?
b. It is a far far better thing I do, than I have ever done.
c. Alas, poor Yorick. I knew him well.

4 If red houses are made out of red bricks and yellow houses are made out of yellow bricks, what are green houses made out of?

5 If on the last day of February 1980—and remember it was a

leap year—you had gone to bed at seven o'clock, having set the alarm to wake you at 8:15 A.M., how much sleep would you have got?

6 An archaeologist recently claimed that he had found a coin dated 46 B.C. Do you think he had?

7 What is it that occurs four times in every week, twice in every month, but only once in a year?

8 Their are five mistaikes in this sentance. Can you spot them?

(See Answers.)

MEET THE PRESS

We all make mistakes, but some of us make more than others. The world's press is rightly noted for its ability to misquote, misprint, and misunderstand absolutely everything. If you've ever had anything to do with an event that's been written up by the press, I guarantee there was at least one error in the report. There's no point in sulking about it: You've just got to face life as it is and make the most of it. After all, misprints like these—all taken from actual newspaper reports—can add a little extra something to a story.

"The landlord insisted that no female should be allowed in the bra without a man."

"Miss Patricia Muddleton, qualified vice instructor, sang *Christian, Dost Thou See Them?* on Sunday night."

"Mrs. Alsop was married before anaesthetics came into use in surgical operations."

"I never went through that ghastly adolescent phrase most girls experience. I went from child to woman in one go. One day I was a child. The next, a man."

"Mrs. Freda Wallace Brown, 79, of Baltimore, Md., dined this week at her home. Service and cremation will be held next Thursday at 2:00 P.M."

"Never throw away old chicken bones, or those left from a roast. Put them in water and boil them for several hours with a few diced vegetables, it will make very delicious soup."

"The bride was gowned in white silk and lace. The color scheme of the bridesmaids' gowns and flowers was punk."

"The accident occurred at Hillcrest Drive and Santa Barbara Avenue as the dead man was crossing the intersection."

"An Arab country, like Ireland, is a place where the remarkable seldom happens, and the impossible is of frequent occurrence."

"Many students are planning to follow the team to the scene of the bottle."

"Mr. Bromsgrove suffered a stroke on 24 November 1980 but with the loving care of his family and his kind and efficient nurse, he never fully recovered."

"The ladies of the Helping Hand Society enjoyed a swap social on Friday evening. Everybody brought along something they no longer needed. Many of the ladies were accompanied by their husbands."

"Over 50 children took advantage of the mobile clinic and were examined for tuberculosis and other diseases which the clinic offered free of charge."

"The new bride is approximately eighteen feet wide from buttress to buttress."

"We note with regret that Mr. Willis Overing is recovering after a serious car crash."

"The new hospital extension will enable patients to be prepared and served in such a way that has previously been impossible."

"Some of the boy's methods are quite ingenious, the professors at the Institute have found. For instance, when asked to multiply 20 by 24 mentally, he gave the answer—600—in a few seconds."

"Sex and violence came into Jane Morgan's life gradually. Then she became a Christian and matters escalated."

"Ms. Turner has set up a campaign against incestuous relationships at the house where she loves with her parents."

"The city which claims to have the largest outdoor mule market in the world recently held a parade of asses led by the governor."

"Blend sugar, flour, and salt. Add egg and milk, cook until creamy in double boiler. Stir frequently. Add rest of ingredients. Mix well and serve chilled. Funeral service will be held Thursday afternoon at two o'clock."

"An off-license was looted and police opened fire after they were stoned."

"Before the girls left the White House, Mrs. Reagan presented each of them with a small engraving of the Execution Mansion to keep as a memento."

"We apologise for the error in last week's paper in which we stated that Mr. Arnold Smith was a defective in the police force. This was a typographical error. We meant, of course, that Mr. Smith is a detective in the police farce, and are sorry for any embarrassment caused."

HITTING THE HEADLINES

These headlines have all appeared in English-speaking newspapers around the world. In my view, each one deserves a Pullet Surprise.

MAN FOUND DEAD IN GRAVEYARD

LOCAL MAN HAS LONGEST HORNS IN TEXAS

PASSENGERS HIT BY CANCELLED TRAINS

BUFFALO SWEPT OFF FEET BY MENDELSSOHN CHOIR

MASSIVE ORGAN DRAWS THE CROWD

HAMM FAILS TO IDENTIFY YEGGS

SISTERS WED BROTHERS HAVE BABIES SAME DAY

POLICE MOVE IN BOOK CASE

UNDERTAKER'S FAILURE—LET DOWN BY CUSTOMERS

20-YEAR FRIENDSHIP ENDS AT THE ALTAR

NEWLY WEDS AGED 82, HAVE PROBLEM

LUCKY MAN SEES FRIENDS DIE

BACHELORS PREFER BEAUTY TO BRAINS IN THEIR WIVES

PRISONERS ESCAPE AFTER EXECUTION

MORE MEN FOUND WEDDED THAN WOMEN

FATHER OF TEN SHOT DEAD (MISTAKEN FOR RABBIT)

DEAD POLICEMEN IN THE FORCE FOR 18 YEARS

"LENORE" ONLY OPERA BEETHOVEN WROTE ON MONDAY EVENING

SENATE PASSES DEATH PENALTY MEASURE PROVIDES FOR ELECTROCUTION FOR ALL PERSONS OVER 17

PROTESTOR TRIED TO SPOIL PLAY BUT THE ACTORS SUCCEEDED

EDITORS BLAME TYPE-SETTERS FOR INAKURATESPELING

Q WITHOUT U

The world of words is full of surprises. For example, if you thought words beginning with the letter Q always had to have U as their second letter, you were wrong. Here are thirty that don't:

qabbala	A system of occult theosophy or mystical interpretation of the Scriptures.
qadi	A Muslim judge who interprets and administers the religious laws of Islam.
qaf	The twenty-first letter of the Arabic alphabet.
qaid	A Muslim local administrator.
qaimaqam	A lieutenant or deputy in the service of the Ottoman Empire.
qanat	An undergound tunnel dug in hills to convey water to plains below.

qaneh	A Hebrew measurement equivalent to 10.25 feet.
qantar	Any of various units of weight in Mediterranean countries.
qasab	An ancient measure of Arabia equivalent to 12.6 feet.
qasida	A satiric poem in various related Oriental cultures.
qcepo	A skin infection.
qebhsnauf	A hawk-headed son of the ancient Egyptian god Horus.
qhat	An obsolete spelling of *what*.
qhwom	An obsolete spelling of whom.
qhythsontyd	An obsolete spelling of *Whitsuntide*.
qiana	The trade name of a washable and wrinkle-resistant fabric related to nylon.
qibla	The direction of the Kaaba shrine in Mecca toward which all Muslims turn in ritual prayer.
qinah	A dirge or lament.

And here are thirty more words culled from a variety of English dictionaries. They all contain the letter Q, but again it isn't followed by a U, except in the case of *zaqqum*, which is the only word in the language that manages to have it both ways.

bathqol	A divine revelation audibly given.
burqa	A loose enveloping garment worn in public by Muslim women.
cinq	The number five in dice or cards.
cinqfoil	Any of several plants.
coq	A trimming of cock feathers on a woman's hat.
faqih	A Muslim theologian versed in the religious laws of Islam.
faqir	A Muslim ascetic.
fiqh	In Islam, jurisprudence based on theology.
fuqaha	A plural of *faqih*, above.
hooqqa	A pipe for smoking tobacco.

Iraqi	A native or inhabitant of Iraq.
iraqize	To make Iraqi in character.
miqra	The Hebrew text of the Bible.
muqaddam	A headman.
nastaliq	An Arabic script used mainly for Persian poetry.
paq	A large rodent of Central and South America.
pontacq	A still wine of the south of France, red or white.
sambuq	A small Arab boat.
shoq	An East Indian tree.
shurqee	A southeasterly wind of the Persian Gulf.
suq	A marketplace.
taluq	A subdivision of a revenue district in India.
taluqdar	A landholder.
taqlid	Uncritical and unqualified acceptance of a traditional orthodoxy.
tariqah	The Sufi path of spiritual development.
trinq	A toast, used in Rabelais's *Pantagruel*.
waqf	The granting of property in trust for a pious purpose.
yaqona	A beverage made from the crushed root of an Australasian shrubby pepper.
zaqqum	An infernal tree with excessively bitter fruit, mentioned in the Koran.
zindiq	A heretic characterized by an extreme religious infidelity to Islam.

RIGHT OR WRONG?

THE FACTS OF LIFE

Can you face facts?

Can you bear to accept that when you thought you were right you were wrong all along?

Can you cope with the news that there is no soda in soda water, that rats don't desert a sinking ship, that Charles Lindbergh wasn't the first man to fly the Atlantic, and that Marie Antoinette of France never said "Let them eat cake"?

You can? Well, then you're probably strong enough to read on and discover how mistaken so many of our most cherished beliefs turn out to be.

There is no soda in soda water. It is charged with carbon dioxide like other "sparkling" drinks.

Rats don't desert a sinking ship. They are unable to predict disaster, and so if a ship happens to sink they will go down with it.

Charles Lindbergh was not the first person to fly nonstop across the Atlantic. He was the sixty-seventh, although he was the first to do it alone.

Marie Antoinette did not say "Let them eat cake." The phrase was attributed to her by those in opposition to Louis XVI and first gained currency thirty years before when Jean-Jacques Rousseau had a princess declare "Let them eat brioches" in a fictitious story of his.

The goosestep is not a German invention. It was introduced by the British Army. A commanding officer devised the step to enable him to see if any of his men were drunk.

An ostrich does not bury its head in the sand when it is frightened or wants to hide. It only does so when it is covering its eggs for protection or searching for food.

Mustard gas is not a gas; neither is it mustard. It is a volatile liquid.

There is no rice in rice paper. It is made from pitch or wood pulp.

Camel's hair brushes are not made from camel's hair but from squirrel's hair.

A pineapple is not a pine or an apple. It is a berry. And a potato is neither a vegetable nor a fruit. It is a root.

Spaghetti did not originate in Italy but came from China. It was introduced to Italy in the thirteenth century by the explorer Marco Polo.

"A red rag to a bull" is meaningless—because bulls are color blind.

The Emperor Nero did not fiddle while Rome burned. Fiddles had not been invented, and at the time of the fire he was fifty miles away at his villa.

There is no scientifically sound reason for baiting mousetraps with cheese. Mice like food of all sorts and have no special preference for cheese.

Chop suey isn't a Chinese dish. It originated in California.

Wormwood is not a wood; neither is it a worm. It is an aromatic plant.

Snakes cannot be charmed by music because they have no ears and are deaf to music. However, they can feel vibration, and so it is possible that they respond to a snake charmer's foot tapping rather than his music.

The centipede doesn't have a hundred legs; it usually has twenty-one or thirty, though some have more than one hundred. And millipedes certainly don't have a thousand legs; very few have more than two hundred.

It's a mistake to say the moon shines. It doesn't. It has no light of its own and so only reflects the light of the sun.

Don't quote me

Can you tell who said what?

1 I can't understand what's holding up our missile program. It's the first time the government ever had trouble making the taxpayers' money go up in smoke.
Bob Hope or Alan Alda?

2 You have to be a Republican to know how good it is to be a Democrat.
Jimmy Carter or Jacqueline Kennedy?

3 Humanity is acquiring all the right technology for all the wrong reasons.
R. Buckminster Fuller or Aleksandr Solzhenitzyn?

4 Hollywood's a place where they'll pay you a thousand dollars for a kiss, and fifty cents for your soul.
Joan Baez or Marilyn Monroe?

5 I'm an instant star, just add water and stir.
David Bowie or Dudley Moore?

6 Love is more important than what we can take . . . Please say with me, three times—Love! Love! Love!
Pélé or Janice Joplin?

7 It takes two to destroy a marriage.
Margaret Trudeau or Bianca Jagger?

8 Today's "fact" becomes tomorrow's "misinformation."
Alvin Toffler or Isaac Asimov?

9 I'm fed up to the ears with old men dreaming up wars for young men to die in.
George McGovern or John F. Kennedy?

10 We all live under the same sky, but we don't all have the same horizon.
Mae Tse-tung or Konrad Adenauer?

11 Macho does not prove mucho.
Germaine Greer or Zsa Zsa Gabor?

12 The world is full of willing people, some willing to work, the rest willing to let them.
Ronald Reagan or Robert Frost?

13 Falling madly in love with someone is not necessarily the starting point to getting married.
Prince Charles or Tricia Nixon?

14 You're never too old to become younger.
Mae West or George Burns?

15 The question isn't at what age I want to retire, it's at what income.
George Foreman or Muhammad Ali?

16 When I was kidnapped my parents snapped into action; they rented out my room.
Woody Allen or Bob Hope?

17 No one's free, even the birds are chained to the sky.
Bob Dylan or Allen Ginsberg?

18 Television has changed the American child from an irresistible force into an immovable object.
David Frost or Laurence Peter?

19 Pop music is the hamburger of every day.
Leonard Bernstein or Pierre Boulez?

20 In your heart, you know I'm right.
Barry Goldwater or Richard Nixon?

(See Answers.)

Who's who?

Can you tell who they're talking about?

1 "As . . . himself used to say, all you need for happiness was 'a good gun, a good horse, and a good wife.'"
John E. Bakeless on Daniel Boone or on Doc Holliday?

2 ". . . 's face ranked with Lincoln's as an early American archetype; it was haunting, handsome, almost beautiful, yet it was irreducibly funny; he improved matters by topping it off with a deadly horizontal hat, as flat and thin as a phonograph record."
James Agee on Stan Laurel or on Buster Keaton?

3 "A glorified headmaster!"
Sir Thomas Beecham on Arturo Toscanini or on Leonard Bernstein?

4 "I'd rather be right than . . ."
Heywood Broun on Calvin Coolidge or on Franklin D. Roosevelt?

5 "He was a foe without hate, a friend without treachery, a soldier without cruelty, and a victim without murmuring."
Benjamin H. Hill on Erwin Rommel or on Robert E. Lee?

6 "There is absolutely nothing wrong with . . . that a miracle cannot fix."
Alexander Woollcott on Moss Hart or on Oscar Levant?

7 "Black history began with . . ."
Eldridge Cleaver on Martin Luther King, Jr., or on Malcolm X?

8 "He wrote so much about the yellow peril that his journalism took its distinctive coloration from the subject."
Richard Armour on William Randolph Hearst or on Joseph McCarthy?

9 "Like most great film makers, he began as an artist, and was gradually overwhelmed by the need to prove himself as a businessman."
Charles Higham on David O. Selznick or on Cecil B. de Mille?

10 "He is Neapolitan by birth and Neanderthal by instinct."
Fred D. Pasley on Al Capone or on Benito Mussolini?

11 "[He] has slain the Indians & flogged the British & . . . therefore is the wisest & greatest man in the nation."
P. H. Magnum on Zachary Taylor or on Andrew Jackson?

12 "He was one of the wild characters of the world."
Ann Sheridan on Errol Flynn or on James Dean?

13 "That obstinate, suspicious, egocentric, maddening and lovable genius of a problem child."
Mary Pickford on Douglas Fairbanks, Sr., or on Charlie Chaplin?

14 "You could throw a hat at her, and wherever it hit, it would stick."
Robert Hopkins on Jayne Mansfield or on Katherine Hepburn?

15 "Instead of working out of phony show-biz 'charm' and cuteness and carefully rehearsed topicality . . . was hitting the late fifties mainline—the sense of smothered rage."
Albert Goldman on Lenny Bruce or on Mike Nichols?

16 "This awful . . . This post-mortem poet. This poet with the private soul leaking out of him all the time. All his privacy leaking out of a sort of dribble, oozing into the universe."
D. H. Lawrence on Henry Wadsworth Longfellow or on Walt Whitman?

17 "I have never met anyone as utterly mean as . . . Nor as utterly fabulous on the screen, and that includes Garbo."
Billy Wilder on Ingrid Bergman or on Marilyn Monroe?

18 "He is like some freak of climate—a tornado, say, or an electric storm that is heard whistling and roaring far away, against which everybody braces himself; and then it strikes and does its whirling damage."
Alastair Cooke on H. L. Mencken or on Walter Winchell?

19 "He was playing . . . all the time, but he was really just a big sloppy bowl of mush."
Stanley Kramer on John Wayne or on Humphrey Bogart?

20 "He's the greatest sexual stooge the screen has ever known; his side steps and delighted stares turn his co-stars into comic goddesses. He's a slapstick Prince Charming."
Pauline Kael on Cary Grant or Tony Curtis?

(See Answers.)

SWEET AND SOUR

SWEET

When Marlene Dietrich complained to a photographer that the pictures he'd just taken of her weren't as good as the ones he'd taken of her when they'd last met, he replied: "Well, I'm ten years older than when I first photographed you, Miss Dietrich." That's what I call a compliment—inspired, instantaneous, ingratiating.

In the middle of the last century a French government clerk, charged with the responsibility of issuing passports, found himself confronted by a woman whose dazzling beauty was unsurpassed in his experience. Instead of noting the details of her height, the color of her eyes and hair, her distinguishing marks, and so on, in describing her, he simply wrote: "More like an angel than a woman."

And there is the more recent story of the young man who was applying for entry to the British naval college at Dartmouth. Asked by the interviewing admiral to name three distinguished officers of the Royal Navy, the applicant replied, "Sir Francis Drake, Admiral Horatio Nelson and . . . I didn't quite catch your name, sir?"

As you can tell, I collect compliments, even when they are paid to others. Here is the cream of my collection:

JOHN SPARROW ON MAURICE BOWRA

Without you, Heaven would be too dull to bear,
And Hell will not be Hell if you are there.

ASTRONAUT SCOTT CARPENTER TO MARLENE DIETRICH

I have been into space. I have been to the bottom of the sea, but I have never been as moved as by you tonight.

JOHN COCTEAU ON BALLET DANCER IDA RUBINSTEIN

She looks like the pungent perfume of some exotic essence.

HENRY JAMES, SR., ON HIS DAUGHTER ALICE

I never saw one so fitted by her grace and playfulness of wit to adorn this life.

HELEN HAYES ABOUT HER MATERNAL GRANDMOTHER

She was one of the last generation of real grandmothers. One of the women who made a special grace of age.

LADY BIRD JOHNSON WRITING ABOUT HER DAUGHTER LYNDA ON HER TWENTIETH BIRTHDAY

One generation after another has depended upon its young to equip it with gaiety and enthusiasm, to persuade it that living is a pleasure. And that's what Lynda Bird does for us.

CHARLES DICKENS TO WASHINGTON IRVING

What pleasure I have had in seeing and talking with you, I will not attempt to say. I shall never forget it as long as I live.

OLIVER WENDELL HOLMES TO JULIA WARD HOWE ON HER
SEVENTIETH BIRTHDAY

To be seventy years young is sometimes far more cheerful and
hopeful than to be forty years old.

WILL ROGERS ON FRANKLIN D. ROOSEVELT

He is the first Harvard man to know enough to drop three syllables when he has something to say.

JOHN ROBINSON, SPEAKER OF THE VIRGINIA HOUSE OF BURGESSES,
TO GEORGE WASHINGTON

Your modesty is equal to your valor, and that surpasses the
power of any language I possess.

NELSON ROCKEFELLER NOMINATING RICHARD NIXON FOR HIS SECOND
PRESIDENTIAL TERM

We need this man of action, this man of accomplishment, this
man of experience, this man of courage; we need this man of
faith in America . . . who has brought us to the threshold of
peace.

ROSSINI ON BACH

If Beethoven is a miracle of humanity, Bach is a miracle of God.

KATE CHOPIN ON FELLOW WRITER RUTH McENERY STUART

Her voice in conversation . . . has a melting quality that pene-
trates the senses, as some soothing ointment goes through the
skin. Her eyes do the rest—complete the charm begun by voice,
expression, and a thoroughly natural and sympathetic manner.
. . . She is a delightful, womanly woman.

JOHN F. KENNEDY ON THOMAS JEFFERSON, AT A DINNER FOR NOBEL PRIZE
WINNERS

I think this is the most extraordinary collection of talent, of human knowledge, that has ever been gathered together in the
White House—with the possible exception of when Thomas Jefferson dined alone.

SOUR

Emerson was right: "Every sweet hath its sour, every evil its good." Inevitably fourteen perfect compliments must be followed by sixteen stinging insults. Here they are:

OSCAR LEVANT ON DORIS DAY

I knew her before she was a virgin.

JANET FLANNER ON SOCIETY HOSTESS ELSA MAXWELL

She has never been any closer to life than the dinner table.

COCO CHANEL ON YVES SAINT LAURENT

Saint Laurent has excellent taste. The more he copies me, the better taste he displays.

TRUMAN CAPOTE ON JACK KEROUAC'S WORK

That's not writing, that's typing!

WOOLLCOTT ON PROUST

Reading Proust is like bathing in someone else's dirty bathwater.

MARK TWAIN ON JANE AUSTEN

Jane Austen's books, too, are absent from this library. Just that one omission alone would make a fairly good library out of a library that hadn't a book in it.

JIMMY CARTER ON BROTHER BILLY

Billy's doing his share for the economy. He's put the beer industry back on its feet.

OSCAR WILDE ON JAMES WHISTLER

Popularity is the only insult that has not been offered Mr. Whistler.

WILLIAM WILDE ON BROTHER OSCAR

Oscar is not a man of bad character; you could trust him with a woman anywhere.

SWEET AND SOUR 237

GRAHAM GREENE ON FRED ASTAIRE

The nearest we are ever likely to get to a human Mickey Mouse.

PHILIP GUEDALLA ON HENRY JAMES

The work of Henry James has always seemed divisible by a simple dynastic arrangement into three reigns: James I, James II, and the Old Pretender.

W. BROGAN ON T. S. ELIOT

Mr. T. S. Eliot, in choosing to live in England rather than in St. Louis or Boston, passed judgment not only on the American scene but indeed on his own fitness to adorn it.

GORE VIDAL ON RICHARD NIXON

He will even tell a lie when it is not convenient to. That is the sign of the great artist, you know!

BILLY WILDER TO CLIFF OSMOND (AFTER HEARING HIM SING)

You have Van Gogh's ear for music.

ART BUCHWALD ON JIMMY CARTER

I worship the very quicksand he walks on.

GRACE SLICK ON TRICIA NIXON

The worst thing a little acid could do to Tricia Nixon is turn her into a merely delightful person instead of a grinning robot.

THERE WAS A YOUNG LADY . . .

There was a young lady named Zanka
Who retired while the ship lay at anchor;
    But awoke in dismay
    When she heard the mate say:
"We must pull up the top sheet and spanker."

A limerick, as you probably know, is a five-line nonsense verse that originated with the eighteenth-century ale-house chorus "Will you come up to Limerick." As a form of poetry it was made famous by Edward Lear.

Although at the limericks of Lear
We may be tempted to sneer
    We should never forget
    That we owe him a debt
For his work as the first pioneer.

The trouble with Lear's limericks is that they tend to be remarkably respectable.

> There was an old person from Twickenham
> Who whipped his four horses to quicken 'em;
>> When they stood on one leg
>> He said faintly "I beg
> We may go back directly to Twickenham!"

And the trouble with respectable limericks is that they tend to be somewhat short on laughs.

> The Limerick packs laughs anatomical
> Into space that's quite economical.
>> But the good ones I've seen
>> So seldom are clean
> And the clean ones so seldom are comical.

I wanted to offer you my choice of the world's top ten limericks, but given that *More Joy of Lex* is designed for family reading, finding ten printable ones hasn't been easy.

> The limerick form is complex
> Its contents run chiefly to sex.
>> It burgeons with virgeons
>> And masculine urgeons
> And swarms with erotic effects.

In making my selection I've done my best to find limericks that are both decent and amusing. After all, in poetry—as in fancy dress—it's subtlety that counts.

> There was a young woman from Aenos
> Who went to a party as Venus.
>> We told her how rude
>> 'Twas to go there quite nude,
> So we got her a leaf from the green-h'us.

If any of the ten I've chosen give offense, I apologize. My sole aim has been "to give delight and hurt not."

> A girl who weighed many oz.
> Used language I dare not pronoz.
>> For a fellow unkind
>> Pulled her chair out behind
> Just to see (so he said) if she'd boz.

There was a young maid from Madras
Who had a magnificent ass.
  Not rounded and pink
  As you probably think—
It was grey, had long ears, and ate grass.

Said an envious erudite ermine:
"There's one thing I cannot determine;
  When a girl wears my coat
  She's a person of note:
When I wear it I'm only called vermin."

Said a cat as he playfully threw
His wife down a well in Peru,
  "Relax, dearest Thora,
  Please don't be angora,
I was only artesian you."

There was a young peasant named Gorse
Who fell madly in love with his horse.
  Said his wife: "You rapscallion
  That horse is a stallion—
This constitutes grounds for divorce."

There was a young girl known as Sue
Who carried a frog in each shoe.
  When asked to stop
  She replied with a hop
"I'm trying to get in Who's Zoo!"

A newspaper man named Fling
Could make "copy" from any old thing.
  But the copy he wrote
  Of a five dollar note
Was so good he is now in Sing Sing.

There was a young woman named Bright
Whose speed was much faster than light.
  She set out one day,
  In a relative way,
And returned on the previous night.

A cheerful old bear at the Zoo
Could always find something to do.
  When it bored him, you know
  To walk to and fro,
He reversed it, and walked fro and to.

God's plan made a hopeful beginning,
But man spoiled his chances by sinning.
    We trust that God's Glory
    Will end up the story
But at present the other side's winning!

U

RSULA WOOP AND FRIENDS

REAL NAMES

Ursula Woop is alive and well and living in East Germany where she recently became National Typewriting Champion.

Adolph Blaine Charles David Earl Frederick Gerald Hubert
Irvin John Kenneth Lloyd Martin Nero Oliver Paul Quincy
Randolph Sherman Thomas Uncas Victor William Xeres
Yancy Zeus Wolfeschlegelsteinhausenbergerdorffvoralternwar-
engewissenhalftschafterswessenschafewarenwohlgepfflegeund-
sorgfaltigkeitbeschutzenvonangreifendurcheinenvanderersteer-
demenschderraumschiffgebrauchlichtalsseinursprungvonkraft-
gestartseinlangefahrthinzwischensternartigraumaufdersu-

242

chenachdiesternwelchegehabtbewohnbarplanetenkreisedrehen-
sichundwohinderneurassevonverstandigmenschlichkeitkonntef-
ortpflanzenundsicherfreuenanlebenslanglichfreudeundruhemit-
nichteinfurchtvorangreifenvonandererintelligenentgeschopfs-
vonhinzwischensternartigraum, Senior, is alive and well and
living in Philadelphia where he has taken to calling himself
Mr. Wolfe + 585, Sr., for short.

The world is full of ordinary people with quite extraordinary names. Here are fifty of them, all alive and well and living
somewhere in the United States, Canada, or Britain.

Eve Adam	Bent Korner
Etta Apple	Joseph Wood Krutch
Philip Brilliant	Hunt A. Lusk
Betty Burp	Spanish McGee
Upson Downs	Asa Miner
Luscious Easter	Savage Nettles
Ophelia Egypt	Belle Nuddle
Alice Everyday	Elly Oops
Wanda Farr	Victor Overcash
Lo Fat	Ure A. Pigg
Thaddeus Figlock	Freeze Quick
Yetta Gang	Wanton Rideout
Solomon Gemorah	Pious Riffle
Bess Goodykoontz	Viola Rubber
Henry Honetchurch Gorringe	Bea Sharpe
Fair Hooker	Bess Sinks
Rutgers I. Hurry	Adelina Sloog
Melvin Intriligator	Verbal Snook
Frank Ix	Daily Swindle
Hannah Isabell Jelly	Ophelia Tittey
Amazing Grace Jones	Brutus Twitty
Love Joy	Viola Unstrung
Evan Keel	Thereon Yawn
Pleasant Kidd	Homer Yook
Royal Knights	Fuller Zest

UNREAL NAMES

Here are the names of thirty-one people who don't exist, except in the fertile imagination of writer Alexander Theroux. In his intoxicating novel *Darconville's Cat*—nominally the story of a young professor who goes South to teach at what we used to call a "girls' school," but the novel is actually an excuse for Theroux to do remarkable things with the English language, reviving words not heard for two centuries and inventing entirely new ones—the author provides a definitive catalog of "real" but unreal names for southern women.

Muriel Ambler	Trinley Moss
Melody Blume	Glycera Pentlock
Ava Caelano	Hallowe'ena Rampling
Wroberta Carter	Isabel Rawsthorne
Barbara Celarent	Cecilia Sketchley
Analecta Cisterciana	Butone Slocum
Ailsa Craig	Millette Snipes
Childrey Fawcett	April Springlove
Galveston Foster	Lately Thompson
Scarlet Foxwell	DeDonda Umpton
Opan Garten	Shelby Uprightly
Marsha Goforth	Martha Van Ramm
LeHigh Hialeah	Poteet Wilson
Elsie Magoun	Rachel Windt
Sheila Manglewurzel	Laurie Lee Zenker
Christie McCarkle	

IDENTITY CRISIS

Edward Banks, Leonard Douglas, William Elliott, Don Reynolds, and Leonard Spaulding are one and the same man: Ray Bradbury. It is not unusual for authors to adopt different pen names for books written in differing styles, but few eminent writers can have assumed as many *noms de plume* as this distinguished gentleman:

Mr. Brown
Groley Byles
Folkstone Canterbury
John Corks
Fitzroy Clarence
Jeames de la Pluche
Frederick Haltamont de Montmorency
Henry Esmond, Esq.
Boldomero Espertero
The Fat Contributor
George Savage Fitz Boodle, Esq.
Major Goliah Gahagan
A Gentleman in Search of a Man-servant
M. Gobemouche
Leontius Androcles Hugglestone
Jeames of Buckley Square
Theresa MacWhorter
Master Molloy Molony
Mulligan of Kilballymulligan
One of Themselves
Arthur Pendennis
Peter Perseus
Harry Rollicker
The Honourable Wilhelmina Amelia Skeggs
Ikey Soloms, Esq., Junior
Miss Tickleboty
Michael Angelo Titmarsh
Lancelot Wagstaff
Theophile Wagstaff
Charles James Yellowplush

What was his real name?
(See Answers.)

SPLIT PERSONALITIES

Showfolk—from Julie Andrews to John Wayne—have been changing their names for generations. Miss Andrews started life as Julia Elizabeth Wells and the Duke was known as Marion Morrison as a child.

Here are the real names of twenty-five more stars of stage and screen. By which names are they better known?

Betty Perske
Benjamin Kubelsky
Edward Israel Isskowitz
Lee Jacoby
Claudette Chauchoin
Frank J. Cooper
Bernard Schwartz
Francesca Mitzi Marlene de Charney von Gerber
Archibald Leach
Harlean Carpenter
Hyacinth Hazel O'Higgins
Roy Fitzgerald
Burl Icle Ivanhoe
Dorothy Kaumeyer
Louise Hovick
Sofia Scicolone
Dino Crocetti
Maria de Carmo Miranda de Cunha
Estelle O'Brien Merle Thompson
Gladys Smith
Virginia McMath
Joe Yule
Mickall Sinott
Shirley Schrift
Sarah Jane Fulks

(See Answers.)

FIND THE MAN

In the wonderful world of anagrams *a gentleman* is *an elegant man,* a *grand finale* is a *flaring end,* and *Adolf Hitler* is very properly *hated for ill.*

Here are anagrams of the surnames of twenty famous men—philosophers, kings, inventors, scientists, statesmen, and so on—from all periods of history. Can you name them:

1	tank	11	onside
2	coat	12	inward
3	linen	13	snares
4	prone	14	uncate
5	loons	15	encase
6	actors	16	pasture
7	radius	17	amusers
8	latins	18	seamers
9	epochs	19	coasters
10	hurtle	20	puritans

(See Answers.)

FIND THE BOY

He'll do in mellow verse is an anagram of *Oliver Wendell Holmes* and a *person whom all read* is *Ralph Waldo Emerson.*

Can you unscramble these words and find fifty first names for boys?

1	rice	8	vane
2	vain	9	raze
3	lark	10	turk
4	lace	11	mile
5	line	12	smile
6	lone	13	irene
7	mail	14	dolly

15 ingle	33 nailed
16 snide	34 wander
17 widen	35 enters
18 cigar	36 lardon
19 nicol	37 sinned
20 lyric	38 flared
21 ducal	39 glared
22 brain	40 monies
23 naiad	41 radian
24 anvil	42 calmer
25 banal	43 events
26 maori	44 arnhem
27 spire	45 ordain
28 sails	46 antrim
29 roped	47 sorbet
30 lynne	48 fasten
31 grade	49 yonder
32 grader	50 meager

(See Answers.)

FIND THE GIRL

Had Indian rig is an anagram of *Indira Gandhi* and *as a man, rejoined old France* is *Jeanne D'Arc, Maid of Orleans*.

Can you unscramble these words and find fifty first names for girls?

1 gem	8 teak	15 dine
2 yam	9 army	16 goal
3 hurt	10 sail	17 coral
4 road	11 lace	18 ladle
5 sore	12 soil	19 daily
6 soar	13 lean	20 canny
7 sets	14 dean	21 inane

22 label	32 ideas	42 breath
23 fared	33 ideal	43 threes
24 Alice	34 Lethe	44 airman
25 Ernie	35 great	45 Easter
26 Lloyd	36 aural	46 monies
27 Lenny	37 Maori	47 Hamlet
28 Aidan	38 amble	48 riding
29 Colin	39 issue	49 triads
30 asset	40 hoard	50 singly
31 lilac	41 osier	

(See Answers.)

COUNTRY NAMES

The names of some countries include within them a boy's or girl's name. For example, the name *Ada* forms part of Can*ada* and Gren*ada*. Can you find names of countries in which the following personal names appear?

1 Guy	8 Philip
2 Stan	9 Mark
3 Dan	10 Ken
4 Don	11 Les
5 Alan	12 Leo
6 Gary	13 Eli
7 Rita	14 Martin

(See Answers.)

O, IS THAT ALL?

Yes, for people whose name it is.

In Burma there are people called U and E, but the most widely used single-letter surname in the world is simply O.

VIOLINISTS ARE UNSTRUNG

Occupational Hazards

Violinists are unstrung.
Bankers are disinterested.
Butchers are delivered.
Models are denuded.
Songwriters are decomposed.
Castles are demoted.
Surveyors are dislocated.
Accountants are disfigured.
Witch doctors are dispelled.
Train drivers are derailed.
Symphony conductors are disconcerted.

Siamese twins are departed.
Diplomats are disconsolate.
Cannibal victims are disheartened.
Ministers are demoralized.
Orchestra leaders are disbanded.
Winemakers are deported.
Mathematicians are discounted.
Advertisers are declassified.
Martians are unearthed.
Admirals are abridged.
Tailors are unsuited.
Neurologists are unnerved.
Brides are dismissed.
Committee members are disappointed.
Electricians get discharged.
Authors are described.
Choristers are unsung.
Mathematicians are nonplussed.
Politicians are devoted.
Calendar makers are disMayed.
Hairdressers are distressed.
Tree surgeons are uprooted.
Prisoners are excelled.
Bridge players are discarded.
Teachers are outclassed.
Turkey stuffers are undressed.
Eulogists are distributed.
Puzzlers are dissolved.
Clubs are dismembered.
Private eyes are undetected.
Botanists are deflowered.
Tennis players are unloved and defaulted!
Arsonists are unmatched and fired!
Gunsmiths, they're just plain fired!

NATIONAL OPINIONS

Hollywood's not-so-eternal triangles usually end up as wreck tangles.

You can always tell a baby from Alabama by its southern drool.

Seeing a brood of children playing outside a teepee on an Indian reservation, a visitor asked the father how many children he had. "Twenty-one," he answered her proudly.

"My, my," said the visitor. "Don't you have endless squabbles and fights and arguments?"

"Not at all," said the father. "We're just one big Hopi family!"

Following a major earthquake in California, a group of citizens set up the San Andreas Fund, which just goes to prove what they say about some Californians being generous to a fault.

A gnome is a resident of one of Alaska's main towns.

Meet the man from Miami! If you think his jacket is florid, you should see his wife's: It's even Florida!

PUN MOTS

Alan F. G. Lewis is the world's premier punster. Here are twenty of his gems:

A Puritan is a man who noes what he likes.

He was like a bull in a china shop until she cowed him.

Slimmer's motto: here today, gaunt tomorrow.

The guru refused to let his dentist freeze his jaw because he wanted to transcend dental medication.

When I'm stoned I get a little boulder.

"You're always telling lice ant you mite n found out," he ticked her off.

The hard part of being broke is watching the rest of the world go buy.

With games like Scrabble you won't get board, but the same's not true of Monotony.

Chalet or shanty? It's a decision we should dwell on.

Banging together brass plates in the orchestra isn't as cymbal as it looks.

Atrophy is a reward for long political service.

I've put my money into a new girlie magazine so I can take accrued interest.

A pessimist is a person who looks at the world through morose-colored glasses.

The chemical name for water is H_2 eau.

Only a fool would milk his company of expenses when none has been in curd.

One man's Mede is another man's Persian.

Pity the poor man who has a big load of debt and doesn't know how to budge it.

The old Christmas spirit is like artificial holly: dead and berried.

I was neutral until a live wire promised me the earth.

The system of decimal notation has its points but fractions are often vulgar.

JESTER STORY

A pun my soul, it can be a dangerous business this punning. Witness the true story of the medieval court jester who was an inveterate punster and punned knight and day until his master, the monarch—an ace of a king and quite a card by all accounts—was driven beyond reason and ordered the fool to be carried away to the gallows, there to be strung up. No sooner had the jester been dragged from the royal presence than the king began to reflect on the problems of acquiring a replacement, and it didn't take long to have him sending a pardon speeding after the condemned jester.

The messenger carrying the pardon reached the gallows

just in time to save the victim, who was already standing with the rope around his neck. The pardon proclaimed the jester's freedom on condition that he never cracked another pun in his life. But old habits die hard, and without thinking the jester promptly said: "No noose is good news."

And they hanged him.

WASHINGTON SQUARE

If you take the surnames of all the Presidents of the United States and try to interlink them in the manner of a crossword you will need a grid with 527 squares. Here it is:

crossword goes here

W	A	S	H	I	N	G	T	O	N																	M
I		O		A																						C
L		O		R			J	A	C	K	S	O	N										P	O	L	K
S		V		F	I	L	L	M	O	R	E		E										I			I
O		E		I		I				F		N	I	X	O	N				C	A	R	T	E	R	N
N		R		E		N			T	A	F	T		N								R				L
				L		C				E				E					J			C				E
		F	O	R	D		O		M		R			D		A	M	O	N	R	O	E				Y
	H					L		A			S		T	Y	L	E	R			H	O					
V	A	N		B	U	R	E	N			D			O					T			N	O		C	
	R		U								I			N		H	A	Y	E	S		S			O	
	D		C		T						S									U		O	E		O	
	I		H	A	R	R	I	S	O	N			T	A	Y	L	O	R				N		V	L	
	N		A		U					N				D									E		I	
	G	R	A	N	T			M		R	E	A	G	A	N		C	L	E	V	E	L	A	N	D	
			A		A			M												T					G	
			N		N					E	I	S	E	N	H	O	W	E	R						E	

WASHINGTON, PENNSYLVANIA

If you study a map of the United States, you will be able to find the names of all but one of the Presidents. For example, Abraham Lincoln is represented by the communities of Abraham, in Utah, and Lincoln, in Nebraska. The only gap is Eisenhower. There doesn't appear to be a community of that name anywhere in the United States, though you can find Ike in Texas.

Finding middle names for all the Presidents isn't possible, and in this respect President Truman presents a special problem. Harry S. Truman was his full name (the S. didn't stand for anything), but since the country doesn't seem to have a town called Harry, let alone one called S, the community of Harrys in Texas has had to serve for both of President Truman's first names. There isn't a town called Jimmy either, and so the thirty-eighth President appears more formally as James Earl Carter.

George (Arkansas)		Washington (Pennsylvania)
John (Kentucky)		Adams (California)
Thomas (West Virginia)		Jefferson (Colorado)
James (Mississippi)		Madison (Wisconsin)
James (Mississippi)		Monroe (Utah)
John (Kentucky)	Quincy (Massachusetts)	Adams (Illinois)
Andrew (Iowa)		Jackson (Mississippi)
Martin (Alabama)		Van Buren (Ohio)
William (W. Virginia)	Henry (Idaho)	Harrison (Georgia)
John (Kentucky)		Tyler (Texas)
James (Georgia)	Knox (New York)	Polk (Nebraska)
Zachary (Louisiana)		Taylor (Arizona)
Millard (Wisconsin)		Fillmore (Wyoming)
Franklin (New Jersey)		Pierce (Florida)
James (Georgia)	-	Buchanan (New Mexico)
Abraham (Utah)		Lincoln (Nebraska)
Andrew (Iowa)		Johnson (Kansas)
Ulysses (Nebraska)	Simpson (Indiana)	Grant (New York)
Rutherford (New Jersey)		Hayes (South Dakota)
James (Georgia)		Garfield (New Jersey)

Chester (Virginia)

Grover (Wyoming)

Benjamin (Alabama)

William (W. Virginia)

Theodore (Alabama)

William (W. Virginia)　　Howard (Rhode Island)

Woodrow (Arkansas)

Warren (Arizona)

Calvin (Illinois)

Herbert (Missouri)

Franklin (New Jersey)

Harrys (Texas)

Dwight (Kansas)　　David (Kentucky)

John (Kentucky)　　Fitzgerald (Georgia)

Lyndon (Vermont)

Richard (Louisiana)

James (Georgia)　　Earl (Wisconsin)

Ronald (Alabama)

Arthur (Nevada)

Cleveland (Ohio)

Harrison (Idaho)

McKinley (Wyoming)

Roosevelt (Oklahoma)

Taft (Kentucky)

Wilson (Connecticut)

Harding (W. Virginia)

Coolidge (Texas)

Hoover (South Dakota)

Roosevelt (Arizona)

Truman (Minnesota)

?????

Kennedy (Wisconsin)

Johnson (Florida)

Nixon (New Jersey)

Carter (Tennessee)

Reagan (Texas)

X!

FOR ADULTS ONLY

You are about to read the shortest poem in the history of world literature. It represents the elegiac cry of the poet—a censorious and half-starved ex-husband at the crossroads of life—when confronted with a plate of ten fried eggs that remind him of his former wife, their honeymoon in Rome, and the happy breakfasts they once shared.

The poem is untitled. Here it is:

X !

BRIEF LIVES

Not so economical but marginally more profound is this little poem that asks a universal question:

> Must
> All this aching
> Go to making
> Dust?

Yes is the short answer.

The shortest poem to encapsulate the whole of human existence is probably this one:

> O life,
> O love,
> O pain,
> O joy,
> O death.

And the shortest single sentence to do the same thing must be this one from *Finnegans Wake* by James Joyce:

> They lived and laughed and loved and left.

I don't think there's much more to be said, do you?

YOUR TURN

IT'S LAUGHABLE

Can you find an everyday English word of eight letters that contains four Gs?

(See Answers.)

IT'S FACETIOUS

Abstemious is a word in which the five vowels *A, E, I, O,* and *U* appear in alphabetical order. See if you can think of thirteen everyday English words containing the five vowels in these sequences:

```
A  I  E  O  U          E  U  O  I  A
O  E  A  U  I          E  U  A  I  O
A  U  I  O  E          I  A  O  U  E
A  I  O  U  E          O  A  U  I  E
E  O  U  A  I          O  U  E  A  I
I  O  U  A  E          U  A  I  O  E
                       U  O  I  A  E
```

(See Answers.)

IT'S POINTLESS

Can you add the necessary punctuation to the sentence below
to make sense of it?

THATTHATISISTHATTHATISNOTISNOTISNOTTHATITITIS

(See Answers.)

IT'S INCOMPLETE

Here are twenty familiar five-letter words with uncommon
endings. Can you supply the missing letters to complete the
words?

```
*  *  R  V  A          *  *  N  O  M
*  *  V  O  C          *  *  X  O  M
*  *  M  A  D          *  *  I  E  N
*  *  U  R  D          *  *  F  I  N
*  *  A  K  I          *  *  M  E  D
*  *  A  P  I          *  *  L  I  O
*  *  O  S  K          *  *  R  I  O
*  *  K  E  L          *  *  L  O  O
*  *  R  E  M          *  *  S  T  O
*  *  X  I  M          *  *  L  V  O
```

Here are twenty familiar six-letter words with uncommon endings. Can you supply the missing letters to complete the words?

*	*	*	O	D	A		*	*	*	G E L
*	*	*	H	M	A		*	*	*	F I L
*	*	*	R	U	B		*	*	*	S U L
*	*	*	H	I	D		*	*	*	T H M
*	*	*	I	O	D		*	*	*	T I M
*	*	*	U	R	D		*	*	*	H O M
*	*	*	E	X	E		*	*	*	X E N
*	*	*	A	L	F		*	*	*	E M N
*	*	*	U	L	F		*	*	*	E B O
*	*	*	Z	O	I		*	*	*	C C O

Here are twenty familiar seven-letter words with uncommon endings. Can you supply the mising letters to complete the words?

*	*	*	*	O C A		*	*	*	*	P O O
*	*	*	*	A R B		*	*	*	*	R Z O
*	*	*	*	N A C		*	*	*	*	V A R
*	*	*	*	U A C		*	*	*	*	H U R
*	*	*	*	F F E		*	*	*	*	T A T
*	*	*	*	R R H		*	*	*	*	U B T
*	*	*	*	O T L		*	*	*	*	O C T
*	*	*	*	I E M		*	*	*	*	T S U
*	*	*	*	Z O N		*	*	*	*	R A X
*	*	*	*	R N O		*	*	*	*	M O X

(See Answers.)

IT'S INCOMPREHENSIBLE

If you can understand that *CCCCCCC* represents the Seven Seas and *EHCA* gives you backache, you should be able to decipher these hieroglyphics.

1 POTOOOOOOOO

2 SYMPHON

3 DNUOR

4 B   E   D

5 BOLT
  TH

6 FECDISTANT

7 REVILO

8 PPPOD

9   C
  GENT
   A

10 ONCE
 9 AM

11 CATN

12 A REMAINDER
    UR
   ———————

(See Answers.)

ZEE END

TOWARD THE END

Toward the end of their lives most people make a will. In his the German poet Heinrich Heine stipulated that in order to inherit his fortune his wife must remarry "so that there will be at least one man to regret my death."

Where there's a will there's often an insight into the life and character of the person whose will it is.

FROM THE LAST WILL AND TESTAMENT OF NAPOLEON BONAPARTE SIGNED AT ST. HELENA ON APRIL 15, 1821:

1 I die in the apostolical Roman religion, in the bosom of which I was born, more than fifty years since.

2 It is my wish that my ashes may repose on the banks of the

Seine, in the midst of the French people, whom I have loved so well.

3 I have always had reason to be pleased with my dearest wife, Marie Louise. I retain for her to my last moment, the most tender sentiments—I beseech her to watch, in order to preserve my son from the snares which yet environ his infancy.

4 I recommend to my son, never to forget that he was born a French prince, and never to allow himself to become an instrument in the hands of the triumvirs who oppress the nations of Europe; he ought never to fight against France, or to injure her in any manner; he ought to adopt my motto—"Everything for the French people."

5 I die prematurely, assassinated by the English oligarchy. . . . The French nation will not be slow in avenging me.

FROM THE LAST WILL AND TESTAMENT OF ALFRED BERNHARD NOBEL SIGNED IN PARIS ON NOVEMBER 27, 1895:

The whole of my remaining estate shall be dealt with in the following way: The capital shall be invested by my executors in safe securities and shall constitute a fund, the interest on which shall be annually distributed in the form of prizes to those who, during the preceding year, shall have conferred the greatest benefit on mankind.

The said interest shall be divided into five parts, which shall be apportioned as follows: one part to the person who shall have made the most important discovery or invention within the field of physics; one part to the person who shall have made the most important chemical discovery or improvement; one part to the person who shall have made the most important discovery within the domain of physiology or medicine; one part to the person who shall have produced in the field of literature the most outstanding work of an idealistic tendency; and one part to the person who shall have done the most or the best work for fraternity among nations, and for the abolition or reduction of standing armies and for the holding and promotion of peace congresses.

It is my express wish that in awarding the prizes no consideration whatever shall be given to the nationality of the candidate, so that the most worthy shall receive the prize whether he be a Scandinavian or not.

Paris, November 27, 1895. Alfred Bernhard Nobel

THE WILL OF ONE WILLIAM HICKINGTON WHO DIED IN 1770:

This is my last will,
I insist on it still;
To sneer on and welcome,
And e'en laugh your fill.
    I, William Hickington,
Poet of Pocklington,
Do give and bequeath,
As free as I breathe,
To thee, Mary Jarum
The Queen of my Harum,
My cash and my cattle,
With every chattel,
To have and to hold,
Come heat or come cold,
Sans hindrance or strife,
Though thou art not my wife.
As witness my hand,
Just here as I stand.
The twelfth of July
In the year Seventy.

Wm. Hickington

THE WILL OF A PHILADELPHIA INDUSTRIALIST WHO DIED IN 1947:

To my wife I leave her lover, and the knowledge that I wasn't the fool she thought I was.

To my son I leave the pleasure of earning a living. For twenty-five years he thought the pleasure was mine. He was mistaken.

To my daughter I leave $100,000. She will need it. The only piece of business her husband ever did was to marry her.

To my valet I leave the clothes he has been stealing from me for ten years. Also the fur coat he wore last winter while I was in Palm Beach.

To my chauffeur, I leave my cars. He almost ruined them and I want him to have the satisfaction of finishing the job.

To my partner, I leave the suggestion that he take some clever man in with him at once if he expects to do any business.

THE WILL OF EDWIN ORLANDO SWAIT WHO DIED IN 1965:

1 I direct that all my creditors be paid except my landlord.

2 I give and bequeath to my good friend, Theodore Weber, my best aluminum tin if I die of anything but indigestion. In that event, I give him a sad farewell.

3 To my old friend, Ann Lewis, I give and bequeath Purcell's "Passing By," which I wrongfully took and carried away last Christmas.

4 I give and bequeath to my dear friend, Mrs. George Hale, the satisfaction of being remembered in my will.

5 To my old pal, Mary Ledgerwood, I give and bequeath the sum of 35 cents. It's not much but it's the beginning of a Scotch fortune.

6 I leave to my lawyer, Huber Lewis, the task of explaining to my relatives why they didn't get a million dollars apiece.

7 I appoint Huber Lewis executor of my will. In view of his profession, I suppose we had better require him to furnish a bond. I give him full power to sell, mortgage or pledge any or all of my estate for the purpose of paying the legacy left by Article 5, and if a sufficient sum cannot be realized, I warn him to be wary of the legatee.

AT THE END

At the end most people have something to say. Few could— or would want to—rival the Famous Last Words of General Sedgewick who peered over the parapet at Spotsylvania and remarked: "They couldn't hit an elephant at this dist————"

The only Famous Last Words that aren't essentially sad are the ones people dream up years before they are going to need them—like these:

GEORGE BERNARD SHAW

I knew if I stayed round long enough, something like this would happen.

RUBE GOLDBERG

Dear God: Enclosed please find Rube Goldberg. Now that you've got him, what are you going to do with him?

ROBERT BENCHLEY

This is all over my head.

ERNEST HEMINGWAY

Pardon me for not getting up.

FREDERIC MARCH

This is just my lot.

CLARK GABLE

Back to the silents.

DOROTHY PARKER

Excuse my dust.

LEWIS STONE

A gentleman farmer goes back to the soil.

HEDY LAMARR

This is too deep for me.

WILLIAM HAINES

Here's something I want to get off my chest.

WARNER BAXTER

Did you hear about my operation?

JEAN HARLOW

Of this quiet and peace
I'm very fond;
No more remarks—"She's a
Platinum blonde."

AFTER THE END

After the end come the epitaphs:

Here lies the body of John Mound
Lost at sea and never found.
Winslow, Maine

Neuralgia worked on Mrs. Smith
Till neath the sod it laid her.
She was a worthy Methodist
And served as a crusader.
Skaneateles, New York

Sacred to the memory of
Jared Bates
who died Aug. the 6th 1800.
His widow, aged 24, lives at 7 Elm
Street, has every qualification for
a good wife, and yearns to be comforted.
Lincoln, Maine

Here lies the body of our Anna
Done to death by a banana.
It wasn't the fruit that laid her low
But the skin of the thing that made her go.
Enosburg, Vermont

Here lies the body of Susan Lowder
Who burst while drinking a Seidlitz powder.
Called from this world to her Heavenly Rest
She should have waited till it effervesced. 1798.
Burlington, New Jersey

Here lies
Lester Moore
Four slugs
from a 44
no Les
no More
Tombstone, Arizona

Here lies
Sidney Snyder
1803–1823
The wedding day decided was,
The wedding wine provided,
But ere the day did come along
He'd drunk it and died, did.
Ah, Sidney! Sidney!

Providence, Rhode Island

To the four husbands of
Miss Ivy Saunders
1790, 1794, 1808, 18??
Here lie my husbands, One, Two, Three
Dumb as men could ever be.
As for the Fourth, well, praise be God,
He bides for a little above the sod.
Alex, Ben, Sandy were the first three's names,
And to make things tidy I'll add his—James.

Shutesbury, Massachusetts

In memory of
Mr. Nath Parks, aged 19,
who on 21st March 1794 being out hunting
and concealed in a ditch was casually shot
by Mr. Luther Frank.

Elmwood Cemetery, Holyoke, Massachusetts

Played five aces
Now playing the harp

Boot Hill Cemetery, Kansas

FINALLY

Let me echo Hilaire Belloc:

When I am dead, I hope it may be said:
"His sins were scarlet, but his books were read."

NSWERS

X MARKS THE SPOT

THE JOY OF LEX

Apoplex, circumflex, complex, Culex, decemplex, duplex, exlex, flex, goo-golplex, hallex, ilex, implex, multiplex, octuplex, perplex, plex, pollex, pro-plex, Pulex, quadruplex, reflex, retroflex, scolex, silex, simplex, supellex, telex, triplex, Ulex, uncomplex

COMPLEX ARRANGEMENTS

Latex, lexicon, excelsior, exclude, dextral, exalted, explode, deluxe, axletree, flaxen, reflexly, sexology, helix, foxhole, lynxlike, extoll, maxwell, explain, explore, relaxed, petrosilex, latexes, phloxes, sexennial, larynxes, plexus, tex-tual, sextile, sextuple, luxes

WHAT'S IN A NAME?

AN ORAL DANGER

The names have been ordered in their so-called alphabetically reduced forms. For example, *Christiaan* and *Christiana* can both be "reduced" to *Aachiinrst*. If all the names are reduced in a similar way, and then these reduced forms are ordered alphabetically, that is the order of my list. Obviously, names with several *A*s come out at the top of the list, and names without any *A*s appear further down the list. Where a set of names has the same number of *A*s as another set, the tie is broken on the *B*s, *C*s, and so on.

VERBIGERATION

1 VV	26 PP
2 CC	27 FF
3 HH	28 NN
4 XX	29 TT
5 WW	30 K
6 Y	31 V
7 JJ	32 C
8 S	33 H
9 GG	34 D
10 KK	35 A
11 MM	36 G
12 LL	37 O
13 AA	38 M
14 Z	39 J
15 EE	40 P
16 DD	41 W
17 BB	42 E
18 OO	43 F
19 UU	44 B
20 SS	45 Q
21 QQ	46 U
22 RR	47 N
23 X	48 I
24 T	49 R
25 II	50 L

MY KINDS OF TOWN

CHICAGO

At least thirty-four, including:

Apkaw	Chikagons
Checago	Chikagou
Checagou	Chikagu
Cheegago	Chikagvv
Chegakou	Chikkago
Cheggago	Chirgago
Chekakou	Psceschaggo
Chicagou	Quadoge
Chicags	Schuerkaigo
Chicagu	Shecago
Chicagvv	Shercaggo
Chicago	Shikkago
Chicaqw	Stktschagko
Chiccago	Tschakko
Chigagou	Tzstchago
Chikag8	Ztschaggo

And just in case it looks as if the typographer has made a few mistakes, let me repeat four of the stranger spellings: *Chicagvv, Chicag8, Chicaqw,* and *Ztschaggo.*

TEEN SENSE IN TENNESSEE

1 San Antonito	11 Savannah
2 Bangor	12 Hudson
3 Casper	13 Los Angeles
4 Pontiac	14 Salem
5 Tucson	15 Denver
6 San Diego	16 Laredo
7 Madison	17 Reno
8 Detroit	18 Las Vegas
9 Notre Dame	19 Toledo
10 Reading	20 New Carlisle

JUST A LINE

1 Graham Greene: *The Power and the Glory*
2 Jean Paul Sartre: *Nausea*
3 Kurt Vonnegut: *Jailbird*
4 Daphne du Maurier: *Frenchman's Creek*
5 Ernest Hemingway: *Fiesta*
6 Charles Dickens: *Bleak House*
7 Franz Kafka: *The Trial*
8 John Steinbeck: *The Grapes of Wrath*
9 George Orwell: *1984*
10 Norman Mailer: *The Naked and the Dead*
11 L. P. Hartley: *The Go-Between*
12 Robert M. Pirsig: *Zen and the Art of Motorcycle Maintenance*
13 Agatha Christie: *Murder on the Orient Express*
14 Jack Kerouac: *On the Road*
15 Frederick Forsyth: *The Day of the Jackal*
16 Virginia Woolf: *The Voyage Out*
17 F. Scott Fitzgerald: *Tender Is the Night*
18 Laurence Sterne: *Tristram Shandy*
19 Gustave Flaubert: *Madame Bovary*
20 Leo Tolstoy: *Anna Karenina*

I BEFORE E?

A FINE SPELL

It's *unbelievable*, of course. And the correct spellings for the other words follow:

accommodation	coxswain
battalion	desiccate
broccoli	ecstasy
calendar	eleemosynary
cemetery	embarrass
Chihuahua	fettuccine
coliseum	gneiss
connoisseur	guillotine

hemorrhage
hypocrisy
idiosyncrasy
jubilee
kwashiorkor
liaison
liquefy
mischievous
moccasin
myrrh
naphtha
occurrence
paraffin
parallel
plausible
pseudonymous
quintessence

rarefy
reconnaissance
renaissance
sacrilegious
sangfroid
shillelagh
subpoenaed
supersede
threshold
ukulele
vermilion
vichyssoise
victual
weltschmerz
Xanthippe
yashmak
zabaglione

CRAZY CROSSWORDS

THE WORLD'S SMALLEST CROSSWORD

PERIOD is the meaning of the clue ACROSS.
DOT is the meaning of the clue DOWN.

AN AUSTRALIAN CROSSWORD

N   O   O   N

AN IRISH CROSSWORD

P   A   T
A   A
T   A   P

As you can see the answer is decidedly apt.

CRAZY CROSSWORDS

A SIBILANT CROSSWORD

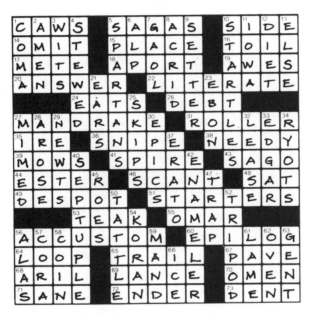

AN ANAGRAMMATIC CROSSWORD

Correct solution first; then intermediate solution of across clues; then explanation of clue.

ACROSS
1 PSITTACINE, ANTISEPTIC (*ant is* + *t* inside *epic*)
6 LANE, LEAN (2 meanings)
10 CONICAL, LACONIC (*con* inside *laic*)
11 MIRACLE, RECLAIM (*rec, 1, aim*)
12 SHRUB, BRUSH (2 meanings)
13 SENESCENT, SENTENCES (2 meanings)
14 INSERTED, RESIDENT (*side in rent*)
15 PRESTO, POSTER (reverse of *ret, sop*)
17 PLATEN, PLANET (hidden stee*p lane t*here is)
19 RINGSIDE, DESIRING (*R.I.* inside anagram of *design*)
23 TURBINATE, TRIBUNATE (*N.A.* inside *tribute*)
25 INTER, NITER (*t* inside reverse of *rein*)
27 ENCLAVE, VALENCE (*Vance,* with *LE* inside)
28 TOILERS, LOITERS (*lo, i, ters* (*e*))
29 TONE, NOTE (2 meanings)
30 STRAIGHTEN, SHATTERING (*hatter* inside *sing*)

DOWN

1 PACES (*p, aces*)
2 IGNORES (anagram)
3 TICK-BORNE (anagram)
4 CELESTE (hidden in reverse of gre*ets elect*orate)
5 NAMING (*N. A. Ming*)
7 ARCHERS (*marchers*, minus first letter)
8 ELECTRODE (*elect, rode*)
9 KRIS (reverse of *sir, k*)
14 IMPATIENT (*I'm, patient*)
16 REGAINING (*E.G.* inside *training,* minus first letter)
18 AFRICAN (*FR I,* inside *a can*)
20 INERTIA (anag. of *I train, e*)
21 INTREAT (former version of *entreat: in, treat*)
22 LATEST (hidden inside stimu*lates t*rend)
24 IRAN (*I, ran*)
26 RISEN (anagram)

A CROSSWORD WITH MISPRINTS

Correct answer first; then correct definition form; then explanation of clue.

ACROSS

1 CLEANER, char, (*C-leaner*)
5 CASTLED, fort (*cast, led*)
9 INFLEXION, bending (*flex,* with *in* first, and *I ON* afterwards)
10 RUN UP, erect, (first letters of Unionist Party after run)
11 BLUFFS, deceives (*b, luffs*)
12 PROVIDER, cater (*ID* inside *p, rover*)
14 INFLATES, swells (*in flats,* around *E*)
15 LEDGE, shelf, (*Led,* first two letters of *geologists*)
18 TWEET, chirp (cf. *tweat, treat*)
20 PRESENTS, shows, (*present, s*)
23 EYEBALLS, stares (cf. *I, balls*)
25 ICE-CAP, cover (*I,C,* reverse of *pace*)
27 MORON, fool (*o* inside *morn*)
28 TRANSPIRE, sweat (anagram)
29 DESIRED, wanted (*sir* inside *deed*)
30 MASSEUR, stroker (*mass,* reverse of *rue,* Fr = street)

Actual answer first; then intermediary answer; then explanation of clue.

DOWN

1 CLIMBS, climes (*c, limes*)
2 EFFLUENCE, affluence (*flu* inside *a fence*)
3 NEEDFUL, heedful (*he,* anagram of *feud, l*)
4 RAID, rand (hidden in I*ran,* dubiously)
5 CONTRASTED, contracted (2 meanings)
6 SHRIVEL, shriven (anagram of *shiver* + last letter in *absolution*)
7 LINED, lived (*devil, reversed*)

8 DEPORTED, reported (2 meanings)
13 STIPULATED, stimulated (*stated*, around I *MUL(e)*)
16 DETECTIVE, defective (*defect* + *I've*)
17 STREAMED, streaked (2 meanings)
19 TRAINER trailer (2 meanings)
21 ENCASES encages (first letter of *ghosts* inside anagram of *seance*)
22 UPREAR uproar (*U* pro *A.R.*)
24 EARNS warns (*n* inside *wars*)
26 FARM, firm (2 meanings)

A FLUID CROSSWORD

P   U   N   C   H

P   U   N   C   H

P   U   N   C   H

P   U   N   C   H

P   U   N   C   H

The crossword is fluid because punch is also a drink made with fruit juices, sugar and spices, often with wine or spirits added. The name comes from the Hindi *panch,* meaning five, the original number of ingredients.

ANGELICAL ASPIRATES

E
TE
ATE
TATE
STATE
ESTATE
RESTATE
PRESTATE

BAA BAA BANANA!

SEEING DOUBLE

A	*bazaar*
B	*ebb*
C	*accord*
D	*add*
E	*fee*
F	*off*
G	*egg*
H	*withhold*
I	*skiing*
J	*hajji* (a pilgrim to the tomb of Mohammed at Mecca)
K	*trekking*
L	*all*
M	*rummy*
N	*inn*
O	*boo*
P	*apple*
Q	*zaqqum* (an infernal tree with bitter fruit)
R	*err*
S	*ass*
T	*butt*
U	*vacuum*
V	*flivver*
W	*powwow*
X	*xx-disease* (a disease of cattle, also called hyperkeratosis)
Y	*gayyou* (a narrow, flat-bottomed boat)
Z	*buzz*

GIRL TALK

1 Marilyn Monroe
2 Golda Meir
3 Martin Luther
4 Franklin P. Jones
5 Socrates

6 Thomas Beecham

7 Myra Barker

8 Sigmund Freud

9 Susan B. Anthony

10 Dwight D. Eisenhower

11 Clare Boothe Luce

12 Erma Bombeck

13 Peter De Vries

14 Gail Sheehy

15 Ronald Reagan

16 Cornelia Otis Skinner

17 Hermione Gingold

18 Jane Fonda

19 Adela Rogers St. John

20 John Kenneth Galbraith

21 Margaret Mead

22 Betty Ford

23 Jacqueline Kennedy Onassis

24 Simone de Beauvoir

25 Fran Lebowitz

INTERNATIONAL SCRABBLE

		WORDS	NO. OF POINTS
1	U.S.A.	GALERES ⎫ with G on the double-letter square	70
	U.S.A./U.K.	REGALES ⎭	70
2	U.S.A.	ELATERS/AE/EL/NA/IT/AE/ER	74
	U.K.	STEALER/ST/TA/EE/AN/LI/EA/RE	75
3	U.S.A.	PARADOX/RAPE/DOILY/OM/XI	173
	U.K.	PARADOX/ZO/EX	153
4	U.S.A.	JOG/OH/GONE	53
	U.K.	ZHO/ZOA	67
5	U.S.A.	JANIZARY/LATHER	115
	U.K.	JANIZAR/JOWL/NOPAL	177
6	U.S.A.	BIOLOGIC/OWED	63
	U.K.	GNOTOBIOLOGICAL/OGEE/OWED/AH/ LAMBLING	684

JARGON FOR BEGINNERS

PREP TALK

A.T.D.	Absolutely to Die. Too much cuteness/nerve/rudeness.
B.M.O.C.	Big Man on Campus. Mr. Prep. A future husband.
C.B.C.	Couldn't Be Cuter. A favorite of girls.
F.T.P.	Falling to Pieces. Useful when you're hinting for a vacation.
G & T	Gin and Tonic. What you drink at the club before, during, and after a tennis game.
H^2	Hot and Heavy. An intense romantic relationship.
H.T.H.	Home Town Honey. That person on whom you cheat while you're away at school or college.
I.B.M.	Instant Big Mouth. Martini—usually used in the plural.
N.O.C.D.	Not Our Class, Dear. He's not for you, believe me. N.O.K.D. (Not Our Kind, Dear) is also heard.
N.T.B.	No Talent Bum. He's only interested in your bank account. Used by women after they've learned the hard way.
O.O.C.	Out of Control. Preceded by any pronoun. Screamed while reeling from too much drink.
O.T.W.	Off the Wall. Mildly crazy, charmingly insane, as in wearing evening dress with Newmarket boots.
P.D.A.	Public Display of Affection. Kissing, necking, sexual relations done outside of one's dorm room or frat room.
R & I	Radical and Intense. Heavy. Great. Defies emphasis.
S.A.	Sex Appeal. What Montgomery Clift had that Mummy liked.
S.O.T.	Same Old Thing. Boring Saturday night. Can be applied to an individual also.
T.B.A.	To Be Avoided. Person, movie, parent, activity.
T.D.C.	Total Design Concept. A house or wardrobe that is thoroughly coordinated. Often used sarcastically.
T.T.F.W.	Too Tacky for Words. Applied to vans with painted sunsets.
U.R.L.	Un-Requited Love. Bittersweet when you are afflicted, annoying when it's someone else.

NEVER SAY DIE

SINGULAR QUIZ

1 axes

2 oxen

3 sons-in-law

4 potatoes

5 piccolos	16 crises
6 attorneys general	17 data
7 lieutenant colonels	18 cannon
8 opera	19 addenda
9 indices	20 agenda*
10 teaspoonfuls	21 phenomena
11 messrs.	22 mesdames
12 men-of-war	23 pelves
13 menservants	24 paymasters general
14 oboes	25 brigadier generals
15 cherubim or cherubin	

*Strictly speaking *agend* is the singular of *agenda,* but nowadays *agenda* is often used as the singular and *agenda* or *agendas* are both considered acceptable as plurals.

PARDON ME!

MY MISTAKE

1 If you copied the proverb down correctly you should have made the mistake of including the *in* twice in succession.

2 Neither is correct. Nine and five equal fourteen!

3 a. If Winter comes, can Spring be far behind? b. It is a far far better thing that I do . . . c. Alas! Poor Yorick. I knew him, Horatio.

4 Green houses are made out of glass!

5 Assuming you do not have a twenty-four-hour alarm clock, you will get just one and one-half hours of rest before the alarm goes off.

6 In 46 B.C. they would have had no idea that Christ was to be born, and so it is impossible to find a coin with that date on it.

7 The letter *e.*

8 The mistakes are: a. *Their* instead of *there.* b. *Mistaikes* instead of *mistakes.* c. *Sentance* instead of *sentence.* d. The fact that there are four mistakes, not five!

RIGHT OR WRONG?

DON'T QUOTE ME

1 Bob Hope	3 R. Buckminster Fuller
2 Jacqueline Kennedy	4 Marilyn Monroe

5 David Bowie

6 Pélé

7 Margaret Trudeau

8 Alvin Toffler

9 George McGovern

10 Konrad Adenauer

11 Zsa Zsa Gabor

12 Robert Frost

13 Prince Charles

14 Mae West

15 George Foreman

16 Woody Allen

17 Bob Dylan

18 Laurence Peter

19 Pierre Boulez

20 Barry Goldwater

WHO'S WHO

1. Daniel Boone

2 Buster Keaton

3 Arturo Toscanini

4 Franklin D. Roosevelt

5 Robert E. Lee

6 Oscar Levant

7 Malcolm X

8 William Randolph Hearst

9 Cecil B. de Mille

10 Al Capone

11 Andrew Jackson

12 Errol Flynn

13 Charlie Chaplin

14 Katherine Hepburn

15 Lenny Bruce

16 Walt Whitman

17 Marilyn Monroe

18 Walter Winchell

19 Humphrey Bogart

20 Cary Grant

URSULA WOOP AND FRIENDS

IDENTITY CRISIS

William Makepeace Thackeray

SPLIT PERSONALITIES

Lauren Bacall	was	Betty Perske
Jack Benny	was	Benjamin Kubelsky
Eddie Cantor	was	Edward Israel Isskowitz
Lee J. Cobb	was	Lee Jacoby
Claudette Colbert	was	Claudette Chauchoin
Gary Cooper	was	Frank J. Cooper
Tony Curtis	was	Bernard Schwartz
Mitzi Gaynor	was	Francesca Mitzi Marlene de Charney von Gerber
Cary Grant	was	Archibald Leach

Jean Harlow	was	Harlean Carpenter
Hy Hazell	was	Hyacinth Hazel O'Higgins
Rock Hudson	was	Roy Fitzgerald
Burl Ives	was	Burl Icle Ivanhoe
Dorothy Lamour	was	Dorothy Kaumeyer
Gypsy Rose Lee	was	Louise Hovick
Sophia Loren	was	Sofia Scicolone
Dean Martin	was	Dino Crocetti
Carmen Miranda	was	Maria de Carmo Miranda de Cunha
Merle Oberon	was	Estelle O'Brien Merle Thompson
Mary Pickford	was	Gladys Smith
Ginger Rogers	was	Virginia McMath
Mickey Rooney	was	Joe Yule
Mack Sennett	was	Mickall Sinott
Shelley Winters	was	Shirley Schrift
Jane Wyman	was	Sarah Jane Fulks

FIND THE MAN

1 Kant 2 Cato 3 Lenin 4 Peron 5 Solon 6 Castro 7 Darius 8 Stalin 9 Cheops 10 Luther 11 Edison 12 Darwin 13 Nasser 14 Canute 15 Seneca 16 Pasteur 17 Erasmus 18 Rameses 19 Socrates 20 Rasputin

FIND THE BOY

1 Eric 2 Ivan 3 Karl 4 Alec 5 Neil 6 Noel (or Leon) 7 Liam 8 Evan 9 Ezra 10 Kurt 11 Emil 12 Miles 13 Ernie 14 Lloyd 15 Nigel 16 Denis 17 Edwin 18 Craig 19 Colin 20 Cyril 21 Claud 22 Brian 23 Aidan 24 Alvin 25 Alban 26 Mario 27 Piers 28 Silas 29 Pedro 30 Lenny 31 Edgar 32 Gerard 33 Daniel 34 Andrew 35 Ernest 36 Ronald (or Roland or Arnold) 37 Dennis 38 Alfred 39 Gerald 40 Simeon 41 Adrian 42 Marcel 43 Steven 44 Herman 45 Dorian 46 Martin 47 Osbert 48 Stefan 49 Rodney 50 Graeme

FIND THE GIRL

1 Meg 2 May (or Amy) 3 Ruth 4 Dora 5 Rose 6 Rosa 7 Tess 8 Kate 9 Mary (or Myra) 10 Lisa 11 Clea 12 Lois 13 Lena 14 Edna 15 Enid 16 Olga 17 Carol 18 Della 19 Lydia 20 Dancy 21 Annie 22 Bella 23 Freda 24 Celia 25 Irene 26 Dolly 27 Lynne 28 Diana 29 Nicol 30 Tessa 31 Cilla 32 Sadie 33 Delia 34 Ethel 35 Greta 36 Laura 37 Moira 38 Mabel 39 Susie 40 Rhoda 41 Rosie 42 Bertha 43 Esther (or Hester) 44 Marian (or Marina) 45 Teresa 46 Simone 47 Thelma 48 Ingrid 49 Astrid 50 Glynis

COUNTRY NAMES

1 Guyana 2 Afghanistan or Pakistan 3 Jordan or Sudan 4 Indonesia 5 New Zealand 6 Hungary 7 Mauritania 8 Philippines 9 Denmark 10 Kenya 11 Lesotho 12 Sierra Leone 13 Belize 14 Martinique

YOUR TURN

IT'S LAUGHABLE

Giggling

IT'S FACETIOUS

Here are the most obvious solutions:

AIEOU	*ambidextrous*
OEAUI	*overhauling*
AUIOE	*cautioned, auctioned*
AIOUE	*anxiousness*
EOUAI	*encouraging*
IOUAE	*discourage, inoculate*
EUOIA	*pneumonia, euphoria, sequoia*
EUAIO	*reputation, refutation, equation*
IAOUE	*dialogue*
OAUIE	*consanguine*
OUEAI	*housemaid*
UAIOE	*ultraviolet*
UOIAE	*unsociable*

IT'S POINTLESS

That that is, is; that that is not, is not; is not that it? It is!

IT'S INCOMPLETE

FIVE-LETTER WORDS

larva, havoc, nomad, gourd, khaki, okapi, kiosk, yokel, harem, maxim, venom, buxom, alien, elfin, cameo, folio, curio, igloo, gusto, salvo

SIX-LETTER WORDS

pagoda, asthma, cherub, orchid, period, absurd, annexe, behalf, engulf, borzoi, cudgel, fulfil, consul, rhythm, victim, fathom, flaxen, solemn, gazebo, stucco

SEVEN-LETTER WORDS

tapioca, rhubarb, almanac, bivouac, giraffe, catarrh, axolotl, requiem, horizon, inferno, shampoo, scherzo, samovar, sulphur, habitat, redoubt, concoct, jujitsu, anthrax, flummox

FLOWER FIVERS

tulip

IT'S INCOMPREHENSIBLE

1 potatoes

2 unfinished symphony

3 roundabout

4 bedspread

5 thunderbolt

6 disinfectant

7 Oliver Twist

8 two peas in a pod

9 undercover agent

10 once upon a time

11 tin can

12 You are under arrest.

About the Author

Gyles Brandreth is one of Britain's most prolific and successful authors, having sold over six million copies of his many books. A dozen of his children's titles have appeared in the United States, and Morrow has published both *The Joy of Lex* and *The Puzzle Mountain*. Since 1981 his weekly "Alphabet Soup" column has been syndicated throughout America and Canada.

Born in 1948 and educated at Oxford University (where he was a Scholar at New College and, like six British Prime Ministers before him, President of the Oxford Union), Gyles Brandreth is also a journalist who has written for most of Britain's top newspapers and magazines, a broadcaster who has made over a thousand appearances on radio and TV, the chief executive of a multimillion-dollar publishing company, a theatrical producer with three London hits to his credit, the founder of the British Scrabble Championships, a former European Monopoly Champion and the holder of the world record for the longest ever after-dinner speech—twelve and a half hours!

He has lived in Hollywood, Baltimore, Washington, D.C., and New York, but now lives in London with his wife, who is also a writer, and their three children, who all have unique English names: Benet, Saethryd and Aphra.

According to the *Scottish Sunday Post*, "Gyles Brandreth is the most likeable genius I've ever met!" According to the London *Daily Mail*, "Gyles Brandreth is the sort of person that a breakfast cereal company would give their right arm for. He's bursting with vigour, fizzing with happiness, sizzling with vim and *Cosmopolitan* magazine once picked him as one of England's most eligible bachelors, though he was actually married at the time." According to the London *Sun*, "Gyles Brandreth is a writer, talker, wit and diversified character with a bowling-over effect on anyone he meets."